The Brave New World of Goan Writing 2018

Anthology

Edited
by
SELMA CARVALHO

Published by BOMBAYKALA BOOKS.
A division of Curato LLP.
1509, Peninsula Park, A-4, Veera Desai Road,
Andheri (West), Mumbai 400053.
bombaykala.com
info@bombaykala.com

Cover design by Ishaan Jajodia.

Contents

Introduction

A sense of exceptionalism permeates the abundant literature of the 20th century Goan. Much like their European counterparts, Goans embraced a *saudosismo* (regret, nostalgia) mourning 'a vision of the past as lost,' (Festino and Melo e Castro, 2017). Their writing, informed by a geographical specificity centred around the '*bhatkar's* mansion' or by extension the Goan village exemplified as an idyll. No murderous rage or extreme emotion resided in the village. These lives were fissured only by their own petty vanities and moralities. Peopled by domineering patriarchs and matriarchs, and put about by tainted bloodlines and tarnished legacies, the antagonists fell on their own sword.

The title of the anthology, *The Brave New World of Goan Writing 2018,* signifies a departure from the comfortable spaces of our parochial past. Goa meanders through these pages but it has been re-imagined: it is domiciled outside of its physical dimension in homelands far away and it has assumed as its own, people whose names don't end with 'kar' or an enunciated Portuguese vowel.

If the contemporary writer succumbs to a *saudosismo* at all, then it is the loss of Mother Earth they mourn. Despite writing independently of each other, separated by time zones and continents, and without the objective of achieving thematic unity, environmental concerns thread through these narratives and metered verse. 'The Bog Bodies of Old Neighbours,' 'Kokum,' 'Forest Sanctuary,' 'The Metamorphosis of Joe Pereira,' the memoir,

'Bombay Blues,' and the poems, 'Kiran,' 'Confluence,' and 'Ghosts,' decry the devastation indiscriminate 'development' has wrought upon the environment and on displaced communities.

'The freshly scarred earth, its scooped out innards swept upon mounds of debris,' 'Now the parapets crumble like stale cake,' 'Because mountains too are equal to men,' 'Violation is always violent,' 'The writing on the wall is clear for anyone to see — a soiled and bruised paradise,' are lines taken from the pens of individual writers and yet, strung together, they tell a coherent story.

By the mid-nineteenth century, large swathes of the Goan population migrated to parts of the Portuguese and British empires, predominantly to the port towns of India and East Africa but also to Burma. Distant people and their histories now became intertwined with our own, seeping in a myriad ways into our consciousness. 'The Thing About Myron,' 'A Dolphin in the Ganges,' 'Matters of the Heart,' 'You Can Never be Too Careful,' 'The Bayingyi People of Burma,' 'Once Upon a Christmas,' 'Young Under the Apple Boughs,' 'The Menino Will Come Tonight,' 'Status: Unknowable,' and 'A Goan in Macau,' speak of these new lands Goans adopted or in same way mirrored life in Goa. They speak to the heart of Goan plurality, of how they shaped us and the debt we owe them.

This anthology is a departure from the old, in its embrace of modernity. In Jessica Faleiro's 'Unmatched,' for instance, the conventional short story with its linear narrative arc has been deconstructed and yet it retains elements of action, conflict and topicality, wonderfully capturing the zeitgeist of our times.

Re-encounters with a defunct lung of Goan literature — that is, Goan literature in Portuguese — revived by the efforts of the collective 'Pensando Goa,' add significantly to the historiography of Goa. 'You Can Never be Too Careful,' was written by Augusto do Rosário Rodrigues, in Portuguese, and appears here as translated by Paul Melo e Castro. In the essay that follows, 'Portuguese Language

Goan Literature: Whence, Whither and Wherefore,' Castro explains the importance of bringing lost texts back into the fold. Everywhere is an awakening that indigenous literature has to become more accessible. Glenis M. Mendonça's essay, 'The Konkani Short Story: Amplifying Unheard Voices,' examines the importance of representing marginalised and missing voices — that of women and the subaltern bahujan community — and reaching a wider readership by translating their work into English.

'The Letters of C. E. U. Bremner: Same Old Tired Prejudices,' drawn from the secret communiqués of Claude Bremner, British India Consul in Goa (1940–1943), provide a new perspective on 1940s Goa.

Concluding the anthology is Jugneeta Sudan's brilliant essay, 'Camões in Goa: The Journey of an Epic,' which looks at modern interpretations of the Homeric *Os Lusíadas*. Sudan's argument that 'intercultural studies involving the epic have opened pathways of understanding and dialogue, and renewed ways of seeing, facilitating a new present,' best summarise how Goa experiences a literary Renaissance every century.

A core principle of the *Joao Roque Literary Journal* is that it reflects Goa's complex, multi-layered history and our inherent liberal values, and this anthology derived from the journal, hopefully fulfils that principle.

Selma Carvalho
Editor, *Joao Roque Literary Journal*

SHORT STORIES

Selma Carvalho is an *O Heraldo Goa* columnist and author of non-fiction books *Into the Diaspora Wilderness* (Goa 1556, 2010), *A Railway Runs Through: Goans of British East Africa* (2014) and *Baker Butcher, Doctor Diplomat: Goan Pioneers of East Africa* (2016). Between 2011 and 2014, she led the Oral Histories of British-Goans Project funded by the Heritage Lottery Fund UK. Her fiction and poetry have been published by *Litro, Lighthouse* and online *Mechanics' Institute Review* (Birkbeck). Her work appears in 12 anthologies and has been translated into the Portuguese for the *Journal of Portuguese Diaspora Studies,* 2018. She has received a nod from numerous competitions, notably as a shortlist finalist for the London Short Story Prize 2017, runner-up for the Dinesh Allirajah Prize 2017 and the Dorset Fiction Award 2018, and winner of the Leicester Writes Prize 2018. Her collection of short stories, *Sisterhood of Swans,* was longlisted for the prestigious SI Leeds Literary Prize 2018 (UK). She lives in London with her husband, daughter and their fat tabby cat.

The Bog Bodies of Old Neighbours

SELMA CARVALHO

Jeorge says, 'Don't do this.'

I smile. 'You're a good son.'

Standing on the precipice, I close my eyes.

I see a fibrous fog rising off an untrammelled road. Mud beaten down to form a path. The path narrows and narrows deeper into an undergrowth assailing me with its thorny vengeance, digging into my skin, bruising it pink, reddening it rough. I see the clearing, a pinhole, a spotlight from the sky. I see the house, its red roof sloping downward with outstretched wings of weathered eaves. There are flowers strewing petals in the gambol between garden and game; strung pearls of jasmine and pods gorged green of marigolds. There are ruffled trees as yet unfruiting but I can tell them by the wingspan of their branches, the flat of their fluttering leaves, the smell of their floating nectaries. How do I know them all?

'Don't do this. You don't belong there,' Jeorge pleads.

He goes to the kitchen cupboard and pulls open a door. There behind the packets of Jammy Dodgers, the jars of thick-cut marmalade and tins of tuna, are boxes of tea. He reaches for a box and reads the label. It says English Breakfast Tea. He brings it with him to the kitchen counter and puts the electric kettle on. He puts a teabag in a sturdy mug and waits for the water to come to boil. He tips the water into the mug, tosses the teabag into the bin, and brings the tea to me.

'Drink this,' Jeorge says, placing the mug in front of me, 'it will make you see reason.'

'Let's drink tea and eat scones,' I scoff.

My eyes close; my lashes are spider legs flickering shut.

I part the green. I walk past strutting stalks and flailing stems. I climb the steps to the house. Ten big stone steps. I am inside the house. I know this house. In here, the world is dark and airless, the windows closed. A frugal filter of light seeps from the roof skimming the surface of bare rooms. I know who lives here. Here the blow is swift onto the flesh and the bruise is silent in the night. Here lives the shadow of hanging hand-me-downs, the frugal jollies of hungry eyes and the plaintive whiny of tied dogs. Where are the children? I can hear murmur-incantations coming from deep within the house as I walk through its rooms. I can smell the woodfire in the kitchen and I know that is where I will find them.

There they are. Within the darkness, fire flares enfold them in a cask of yellow, huddled over a boiling pot, smaller it seems than their distended bellies. The tall girl is preparing the evening gruel. The other three, too young to assist, are crowded around her rail thin body. In a few years, the tall girl will vanish into the fog of a hopeless marriage, ripped apart from her childhood sweetheart, shipped across the seas to suffer the limp affections of a fatherly man. But the other three, they will go on to have better lives because she will send home money.

And now the house turns on its axis and inside a warren of sunlit rooms, scatter shambling bell-shaped aunts, inebriated uncles and rambunctious cousins running riotous circles. Here the harsh word slips from spiteful lips onto ears curling with ever present resentment; decades of wasteful feuds rest as if in a graveyard, putrefying; egos are jellied with misguided conceit; and idle chatter falls like dappled afternoon light, blotting into darkness. Here, the lace curtains close tightly on frivolous lives.

I break free from the house. I am running, running through the paddy fields. I can smell the grain and the husk all around me, the upright stalks brushing against my skin like sandpaper, stagnant water lapping low at my ankles. And still I'm afraid that I will drown, carried over the mud banks, through the sluice gate and into the river. I see it then, the water snake slithering towards me. I scream and scream, and a hand, calloused and strong, young but already weary, pulls me out. It is my cousin who rescues small, trapped birds, mending their beaks and claws, and releasing them back into the wild.

I see him again and he is dead. I see him in his coffin, being carried by young men wearing white shirts and black arm bands, who, after lowering him into the ground, retreat to the local tavern to play carrom, drink the local brew and chew on tobacco. There by the ghastly light of the diesel Petromax hanging low on the wooden beam, men slide into a slurry pit of decomposition.

I fly over a chapel; small, dark and painted blue. The people, they sit so close together, breathing in the redemptive fumes of collective supplication. They close their eyes and fold their hands, and they pray; for outside the chapel are barren lives unfolding, laden heavy with debt, crop failure, alcohol, gambling and disease. Small dreams birthed by docile hearts which shrivel on trees unable to fruit. Dreams preserved in songs of love and loss and faith but never protest.

But there is the local vicar in all his parochial Catholic glory, in vestments of resplendent white and a mane of embroidered gold. He drinks deeply of the shinning chalice and tells them to trust in a colonising God. The lean-cheeked altar boy coughs and the choir in the loft sing hosannas to the Lord. The old choir master swings his stump baton and shifts his limp leg; he directs the congregants to a hailstorm of alleluias, the likes of which I've not heard before.

'Let it go,' Jeorge urges me again.

He says, 'Look, there's the box you put aside for Barnardo's. We can drop it off on Saturday. I'll drive you there.'

Yes, there is the carton of things I don't need, safely stored in a corner. I am a good person. I give to Barnardo's and volunteer at the

Red Cross. I tick the appropriate box and vote at local elections. I segregate my waste. I recycle paper and glass. I pay my taxes. I swear allegiance to my first world country. I am the good immigrant.

I close my eyes and I am back.

I'm standing where congregate a few houses. The mango tree and bougainvillea at the window stretch their limbs to scale the walls but the undergrowth has turned sparse; the earth is thin and timorous. The digger and the scrapper and all things sharp-edged have been this way. I can smell the freshly scarred earth, its scooped out innards swept upon mounds of debris. I see the fissures on the walls, the peeling skin of paint, the broken tiles, the shattered glass, the perforated line between despair and abandonment. I know the hive of souls who evaporated from these houses because they were hungry, because they had young to feed, and they dissipated into a world far away. Their ghosts cluster here searching for the lives they left behind but the digger has rooted out more than just clumps of earth.

I'm falling from the sky. I'm falling back to earth.

'Stop this,' Jeorge says, 'you aren't responsible for what happened. You had to leave. Just like the others, you had to leave to survive. And you did survive. You're here.'

I'm here! The gargoyle eyes of guilt staring at me; crumbling defences burying me. I should have stayed in that tiny village with its bougainvillea of white and purple, but I left. And I'm here now, drinking English Breakfast Tea and waiting for the washing machine spin cycle to come to end, mourning an irreconcilable loss, wanting to return to a time preserved in peat, peopled with the wakeful bog bodies of old neighbours.

Jessica Faleiro lived in Kuwait, Mumbai, Miami, Paris and London before moving to Goa, where she currently resides in a one-bed writing-studio so that she can hear herself think. She categorises herself as a global nomad and a typical adult 'Third Culture Kid.' Her fiction, poetry, essays and travel pieces have been published in *Asia Literary Review, Forbes, Indian Quarterly, IndiaCurrents, Coldnoon, Joao Roque Literary Journal, Mascara Literary Review, Muse India* and the *Times of India* as well as in various anthologies. Her first novel *Afterlife: Ghost Stories from Goa* (Rupa, 2012) is about a Goan family and their 'ghostly' encounters and she recently released *The Delicate Balance of Little Lives* (2018), a collection of interlinked stories about five middle-class Goan women trying to cope with loss. She won the *Joao Roque Literary Journal*'s Best in Fiction Award 2017 for her short story 'Unmatched.' Jessica worked for Kingston University Press as a sub-editor. She co-edited the March 2018 issue of the *Joao Roque Literary Journal*, titled 'Goa and its Worlds: A Literary Journey', curating writing from the Goan diaspora. Jessica has an MA in Creative Writing from Kingston University, UK. She muses about creativity and runs creative writing workshops.

Unmatched

(In Ten Parts)

Jessica Faleiro

I.

Hi Smitha. Ashish here.

Hi Ashish. Nice to connect. I like your name.

Thanks :-)

Ashish, if you don't mind my asking, who is the little girl in your profile pic?

That's my daughter Priya. She's six.

Are you divorced?

I'm married.

So what are you looking for on this online dating app?

I want to connect with new people, outside my normal circle. I'm not looking for flings.

Ok. Have you connected with any so far?

Yes, I've met a lady with a carbon footprint reducing business, an IT consultant who moonlights as a tarot card reader, an artist, a professional storyteller ... these are not the kind of people I would meet in my usual social circle.

You're the first person I've come across who uses the app in this way!

It lets you develop a friendship on your terms and at your pace.

Is your wife also using the app?

No, but she knows I'm using it to connect with people.

Does she realise you're only connecting with women?

:P I don't think she realises it's a dating app!

Hmmm … so you left out telling her that little detail? :P

There's no need. There's no password on my blackberry. She's free to check my phone and messages anytime.

Oh. Ok.

So Smitha … do you want to meet up for a coffee sometime? I'm free after I drop my daughter off at school in the mornings.

II.

hi what's your star sign smitha?

Leo. What's yours?

aquarius … that's interesting

What? Does that mean something?

fatal attraction ha ha

You're drawing that conclusion based purely on our star signs?

na … na … it's obvious … you liked my photo … na?

So?

we both liked each other's photo and swiped right … means there's an attraction at some level, na?

I would need to get to know you better before I could say that.

ok, so I can come to Goa one weekend? … you live alone?

Slow down buddy! I've just connected with you online and you're inviting yourself to Goa already?

means … ? you gave me your number and we're on whatsapp na?

I gave you my number so we could whatsapp because you have an interesting profile and some similarities — you're also a traveller and into movies, like I am. Plus you have a professional background as a consultant and a Master's degree from IIM — and also because the dating app has such bad connectivity and a slow response rate.

okkk

Are you married?

divorced

Ok, for how long?
since 2012
Any kids?
no, thank God
So what are you looking for from this app?
connect with friends, but hoping for a long-term relationship with
someone like-minded. What about you?
Yes, the same.
smitha … hope you don't mind … but I want to ask you a question
Ok, go ahead.
do you know anything about bdsm?

III.
hi madm you want be serviced?
I don't understand…?
i am profesnal gigulu also givin messeges

IV.
hi smitha. did u like my pic?
Yes Mohan, seems that you've travelled a lot around India?
yah, I luv going round with my Enfield … hopefully you can join me
sometime.
Am still getting to know you.
okkk so what u lookin 4 in a guy?
**Someone who is capable of having an engaging conversation and
with some common interests…**
Okkk … good … dat's me! :-)
:-)
hav u had dinner?
…? Yes
what did you eat?

V.

Hey Ahmed. I've enjoyed chatting with you. Would you like to meet up for coffee sometime?

Yeah, sure, definitely! One thing I want to check with you.

Ok, go ahead.

Can I bring my wife?

You didn't mention before that you are married!

Yes, actually, we are looking for a third person to join us. If we all like each other, then we would like to make it a regular thing.

VI.

Shailesh, thanks for swiping right. It's been good chatting with you. But, I'm curious about what you're looking for on this app. There's an age difference of more than ten years between us.

Yes, I like older women.

So, have you connected with older women before?

Yes, as friends. I feel that they really understand me and are more accepting and patient. Also, I am a virgin and I feel that an older woman would have more experience to guide me in the bedroom. I want to ensure that when I get married I know what I am doing so I can keep my wife happy.

VII.

11.45pm: hey!

11.46pm: are you online?

11.48pm: motu!

9.35pm (+1): Are you calling me Motu?

it's just a pet name.

For whom? You don't know me well enough to be this familiar. We only connected yesterday afternoon and haven't even exchanged phone numbers and you're giving me a pet name?

arre chill yaar! sorry if it was offensive.

VIII.

Hey Deepak, it's been good chatting with you. I need to leave to do some errands. Keep in touch.

Ok, before you go … just curious. Are you married?

No, I am single. Are you married?

Yes.

Then what are you looking for on this site?

A compatible sexual partner.

What do you mean by compatible?

Someone who understands me, who I can talk to, share life's ups and downs with me. Basically, someone who is on the same wavelength as me.

IX.

So what are you looking for in a guy?

At this point Stephen, I'm looking for someone single.

Ha. Don't worry. I'm single. I know what you mean.

Why? Do you find lots of married women on the site?

Yes! Married, separated, bisexual, couples looking for a threesome — all getting in touch with me. But one thing I like about people here, they're pretty upfront and honest about what they're looking for.

True. So, what are you looking for?

Hoping to connect with someone with whom I can have a decent conversation and hopefully, a long term relationship. Also, I love to travel but hate travelling alone or rather, I should say, I'm tired of it.

Do you travel often?

Yes, for work. Been to five continents so far ;)

:-) What else do you look for in a woman?

Well, basic stuff really. She should know what to say and when to keep quiet, especially around my business associates. I like a woman who knows what to wear outside and inside. She should love giving blowjobs. Also, I'm a pretty romantic guy. I'd love to buy my woman lacy underwear. Do you like lingerie?

X.

Hi Jaswinder. I hope your weekend is off to a great start!
Yes, thanks Smitha. How's yours going?
Been hectic so far. Just chilling in front of the TV now.
What are you watching?
Friends.
Which channel?
Comedy Central.
Cool. I love this episode.
Me too :-)
I really liked your pic. Especially the one of you in the red dress.
Thanks. That one was taken in Dubai.
You're a really beautiful lady. Have been hoping to connect with someone like that — smart, pretty.
Thank you. So, what are you looking for on this app?
Hoping to meet someone I can share my emotions and feelings with. What about you?
Same here. Are you single or divorced...?
Am married. But my wife is in USA. In Seattle.
So you're not able to share your emotions and feelings with her?
We're both busy. You know how it is. Life. Am pretty lonely.
Then why don't you live in the same place?
She didn't give me a choice. Just got a job she couldn't refuse, packed a suitcase and left. We speak on the phone, but it's not the same.
Hmm
Smitha, don't you get lonely sometimes?

Roanna Gonsalves was born and brought up in Mumbai, and attended St. Xavier's College. She moved to Australia in 1998 as an international student. She is the author of *The Permanent Resident* (UWAP, 2016) published in India as *Sunita De Souza Goes to Sydney* (Speaking Tiger, 2018). Her book won the prestigious NSW Premier's Literary Awards Multicultural Prize 2018, and was longlisted for the Dobbie Literary Award 2018. It is on several lists of must-read books, and on the syllabi of courses at a number of universities. Her work has been compared to that of Alice Munro and Jhumpa Lahiri. Roanna's four-part series of radio documentaries, *On the Tip of a Billion Tongues,* commissioned and broadcast by Earshot, ABC RN, is an acerbic socio-political portrayal of contemporary India through its multilingual writers. She is a recipient of the Prime Minister's Australia Asia Endeavour Award, is co-founder and co-editor of *Southern Crossings,* and has a PhD from UNSW. She has been an invited keynote speaker and guest at several writers' festivals, and is a well-regarded workshop facilitator. She is still looking for that perfect *bhelpuri* in Sydney.

The Thing About Myron

ROANNA GONSALVES

The thing about Myron is not that he has a daughter. God knows, I have two sons myself. If anything, the reality of children has ensured that we understand each other's priorities and shelter each other's vulnerabilities. It's not that he lost his job or, rather, was pushed out by the latest round of university rebranding, and has begun to work in high schools as a substitute teacher. Teaching in high schools seemed to be the dependable path for a burnt-out academic like him, his jazz standard of employment options, when the neoliberal university had sneezed its final sneeze in his face. It's not even that he's fallen hook, line, and sinker for the South Asian Australian Catholic Association, SAACA we call it, although it is 99% full of Goans, with a sprinkling of Mangaloreans, East Indians, and the odd Anglo from Bangalore — the original one percent.

The thing about Myron is that while our paths may have crossed as if ordained by the mythical man in the sky himself, our bodily questions asked and answered, the fingers of reason touch us in incompatible ways.

The thing is, Myron is quite mainstream, glancing at a variety of sources but backing only those that have popular purchase. It must be the result of countless years in a university, back to the wall, eyesight failing, and the realisation that the best self care would be to go with the flow, give the bastards only what they want.

I am here, sitting in my car, across the street from his house, waiting for the rain to stop so I can make a dash for it. I can't put the windows down but I can sense the wet earth, like the last rains on the paddy fields around the church at home, before the builders doused them with concrete and then lit a different match.

I have also joined SAACA after those issues with Peter and Marina Soares who were hell bent on cutting corners. No, I have no problems with SAACA. In fact, I have offered to redesign their logo for free. I may be a highly experienced nurse, but I'm also a prize-winning artist. Their current logo and colour scheme is, how shall I put it, fresh off the boat, coir brown against a watery bougainvillea pink. I meant that metaphorically, of course. I'm quite aware of what can and can't be said, all the shoulds and shouldn'ts of this world that have earned their place.

Yesterday, when I asked Myron if he wouldn't mind bringing me some of his famous egg masala for breakfast on the 26th morning — we could eat it together at the park, under the Port Jackson fig, just before the Survival Day Rally — I didn't foresee this particular turn of events. I thought I'd go straight to Redfern after my night-shift in the Cardiac Unit.

He said, 'Er.'

That hesitation, when I was expecting nothing but a confirmation of plans, was enough to make the molecules around us shift and widen the space in our togetherness. It was not the kind of space that Kahlil Gibran advised, but a more sinister gap, like that between a platform and a train that was leaving it without schedule.

We only met last September. In many ways we are still tourists in each other's cities of the mind, still admiring the vistas at each turn of the self, still unsure of the way.

January 26 is Republic Day in India. It is fairly non-controversial for mainstream Indians who, ironically, don't sully themselves with the Dalit question while celebrating a day that's actually only worth celebrating because of the foundational work of Babasaheb Ambedkar. The narrative of native self-government is triumphant while the bouncers at the national gates kick out alternative stories. Likewise in Australia, the mainstream account of the arrival of the First Fleet, the founding of White Australia on January 26 gyrates with impunity, with blessings, in fact, from all manner of government. They call it Australia Day. The Aboriginal and Torres Strait Islander people, and other intelligent Australians, call it Invasion Day, or Survival Day.

So when Myron said 'Er,' I assumed he hadn't heard me properly.

'The Survival Day rally,' I said. 'I thought I'd go there straight after work, after the night shift.'

He was chopping onions while I sat on his sofa for two hours of respite before going home to cook dinner for the kids.

He stopped chopping, put the knife down, half the onion uncut. Now that's a gesture that indicates a seriousness of purpose, an intention to grasp the weight of the moment and to grapple it with honour.

He went to the music system and turned on Miles Davis and John Coltrane playing the slow and certain 'Some Day My Prince Will Come.'

To be honest, I would have preferred their emphatic reclamation of 'Bye Blackbird.' But Myron and I were not yet fully in accord with each other's likes and dislikes, so I didn't say anything. Instead, I waited for him to layer the now turbulent, now placating saxophone and trumpet with words of his own.

'I usually take Priya to the Australia Day Fun Day at our park. It's organised by our Council. She just loves the Jumping Castle, the gözleme stall, the free native saplings they hand out.'

Was he pulling my leg? Was he being ironic? Was this a test? Nothing in his tone, in his manner these past few months, indicated ignorance.

'You go to the Australia Day Rally?'

'Don't you?'

The CD skipped and gave us momentary pause.

'I used to go,' I admitted, 'when I was new here, and all I knew about this country was that the houses on our street looked exactly like the houses in Salvador Do Mundo. Made me feel more at home. But that position has become untenable now. I thought you …'

'Of course I'm aware of all sides of the debate.'

Now this really pissed me off.

'There are no sides to the debate. It's Invasion Day. It's the day this continent was invaded, land taken from the custodians. It's Survival Day. They have survived despite …'

'I know. I know.'

He washed his hands, and came and sat down next to me.

He put his arm around my shoulders.

To flinch would be to draw unmistakable battle lines. To stay still would demonstrate passivity.

I put my hand on his.

On the CD, the piano and drums were given some space to shine.

'As immigrants, as beneficiaries of indigenous oppression, we have a duty to pay the rent on this country,' I said.

He yanked his hand out of mine.

I was surprised at this sudden turning of the tables. I may have sounded as righteous as a vice-chancellor. I was supposed to decide when and how to bruise, not allow him that power.

Then he said, 'For God's sake don't lecture me on the duty of the immigrant. I make a monthly donation to the Indigenous Literacy Foundation. Do you? Tell me, do you?'

I didn't expect such an outburst from Myron, although I should have seen this coming, this inclination towards vulgarity, this inability to maintain a regard for truth and propriety, despite him being an art historian, this loss of control.

Just last Saturday, we were at Woolies doing our groceries, laughing at the vindaloo paste and the Goan fish curry paste now being sold in pretty packages to non-Goans, not unlike our homeland itself. Myron picked up a packet of flushable cleansing wipes.

'For my daughter,' he said, 'something soft to wipe her bum with.'
The air was filled with the tube-lit and silent fury of shoppers
having to listen to the Woolies jingle that played unceasingly:
Woolworths the fresh food pee-pearl
'Seriously?' I asked. I wasn't querying his tendency towards
parental overcompensation, which was unattractive but not parasitic.
No. I was more concerned about his nonchalance towards the
environment. 'They're not fully biodegradable, according to a recent
study. Think of the fish being choked with such debris, the islands of
waste floating around the Caribbean. Think even of burning rubbish,
like they do back home, the toxic fumes this produces.'

The way he looked at me that moment was disconcerting, as
if something had just occurred to him about me, as if, all these
months, I had concealed a pertinent fact.

Another shopper accidentally bumped into my trolley and this
broke the tension between Myron and me. The speakers played
the Woolies jingle again and again as if to warn us that everything
new will be old again, inescapable Fibonacci sequences overstaying
their welcome.

Woolworths the fresh food pee-pearl
Woolworths the fresh food pee-pearl

He put his arms on my shoulders as a protective gesture in
front of the other shoppers, and steered me away towards the Pet
Food aisle. But I instantly recognised the river rising up to redraw
boundaries of its own choosing. I couldn't unsee his look upon me.
It unsettled me because I knew what it signalled. It mirrored the
way I looked at him on our second date.

We met on a night in spring, and after that initial post-coital
ease, laden with the imprecise expectations that accompany the first
few breaths of love, we decided to take the next day off work and
go for a long drive. Our kids were safely in their respective schools.
The Bureau of Meteorology predicted rain. A monsoon drive, we
thought, with hot chai somewhere, and deep-fried onion *bhajias,*

replicating the best things about home but without the aggravation.

It rained so hard that visibility on the road was extremely poor. The windscreen wipers were furious but no match for the torrent, as if of retribution, that nature was unleashing upon us. We had to get off the motorway quickly. The first thing that came up was a McDonald's. It was crowded but we managed to get seats away from the toilets.

'Number 156.' That was our order. Two coffees and four hash browns.

To be fair, the boy at the counter — I wouldn't call him a barista — did froth the milk with confidence. But oh, the coffee! Like Waterbury's Compound without the sweet tingling down the spine. I sipped it slowly anyway, appreciating the hot, if disgusting, liquid going down my throat.

Neither of us were game to try the tea. Coffee is the disinterested choice of the desperate driver. A cup of tea, on the other hand, is like a best friend. It is extremely difficult to accept an imitation.

'I'm so glad we met,' he said, holding the cup slightly away from his mouth, as if about to say more.

'Number 160,' the boy announced. The man at the next table got up to leave and threw his used serviettes on the floor. I wanted to call out after him but you have to pick your battles and this was far from a moment to fight. I re-focussed my gaze upon Myron.

'I know I've said this a million times already. It was so fortuitous, our meeting, it changed my life.'

I began to preen inwardly, clarity still elusive, expecting the inevitable paeans to my beauty, my body, my brains, and a final concluding statement that tied together the key points of the argument and extended it with unbridled adulation. I began to form words of reciprocal praise on the tip of my tongue.

'Number 180.' They were moving fast, that's for sure.

'You know, my daughter is also an artist, just like you. She loves to paint.'

'That's really good,' I said, not particularly taken with this reminder of our responsibilities that were supposed to be contained at a time such as this.

'I wanted to ask, have you …'

His eyes had an intensity that comes only from being ravenous, his body attuned to mine. If he was going to ask if I had ever painted my gorgeous self I would have to impress upon him my disregard for vanity. There is a long tradition of self-portraits in the history of art. Surely he would champion the importance of minority self-representation in this long night of the white patriarch. So, no, I would have to insist that my self-portraits were political statements rather than narcissism on canvas, however violently he might praise them.

'Number 181.'

He was still hesitating. I suppose men these days are unsure of how to compliment a woman, what is acceptable and what is not, especially in a place like McDonald's off the Hume. The growl of trucks, without intonation and stress, underscored my anticipation as they turned into the servo next door.

'I wanted to ask, have you, do you have any tips for an aspiring artist, ways to improve her marks in art class, now that, you know, you've won the Parkinson Prize and all?'

'Number 182.'

'I've tried my best to help her, but I'm not a practitioner myself. If you have any advice, I'd be most …'

I knew a mountain had moved somewhere, a curtain had been torn down at noon, the flutter of a butterfly's wing in Vamona Navelcar's studio reverberating here in this caesura between us.

'Number 182, Number 182, anyone here for Number 182?'

I felt like sighing but decided against it in the nick of time, a split-second feat I would never manage to repeat again. This was it. The nub of attraction distilled down to nothing more than the possibility of free greenhousing tips for the offspring. Such a pathetic display of aspiration. Such a pathetic time and place to show it.

'Yeah, sure. Let me think about it,' I said, making sure to leave all inflections of sarcasm at the door. It is possible that my face betrayed my disappointment. I tried to mask it in a most Anglo-Saxon way, by falling back on the weather.

'Oh look, it has stopped raining. Shall we head back home?'

I decided to give it a shot, this relationship that emerged unexpectedly. Three months later we were at Woolies, his look widening the crack under my legs. I needed to summon all the strength in my quadriceps and hamstring muscles, and hurl myself to one side immediately.

Woolworths the fresh food pee-pearl
Woolworths the fresh food pee-pearl

The pet food aisle held no attraction for us urban South Asians wary of non-humans. The music on the loudspeaker stopped abruptly and a less melodic if equally unalluring announcement took its place on repeat.

Please finalise your purchases. This store will be closing in five minutes.
Please finalise your purchases. This store will be closing in five minutes.

Before I knew it I was at his house again three days later, my own personal Paschal Triduum complete, asking about egg masala for Survival Day.

He had just questioned me, me of all people, about my commitment to Indigenous reparation, asking me if I donated to the Indigenous Literacy Foundation. As an insistent Miles Davis filled the room, I heaved myself to full height in my imagination and said, 'Throwing money to our Indigenous sisters and brothers in the privacy of your own home is hardly the same as showing up on the street, putting your body on the line for justice.'

'You've got to be kidding. Money talks. Money walks. You people talk about reparation. What else is reparation if not money?'

We both knew we had crossed a line. I would have taken back my tone if I could. He looked like he too regretted this exchange.

At least he wasn't like the other Indians who didn't know and didn't care about whose land and whose labour they were squatting on, who insisted on maintaining the fiction of the model minority. We were on the same side, more or less. But I would stand by my words. Also, I had no time for patronising rhetorical questions when I was in this for love. The Coltrane solo energised me.

'Reparations by the state. There are different kinds of reparations. Bodies on the ground is the only way to affect change,' I said.

'So individual contributions don't count, in your book?'

'Anonymous individual contributions to one organisation. What about the bigger picture?'

'I prefer to start small and go in hard.'

'That's the safe way out. Visibility on the street is the only thing that sends a message loud and clear.'

'So you think I should stop making a financial contribution, and come and join you on the street?'

I didn't like his disdain. My ancestors did not survive colonisation, the Inquisition, invasion, immigration, flood, famine, financial ruin, the miscarriage of babies and justice, and the paradox of an all-male Mother Church, just so I would have to harbour this higgledy-piggledy blurring of boundaries at the start of a relationship. I would make my position clear.

'Why can't you do both?'

'Why can't YOU do both?'

An intake of breath in the silence of our hearts. We sensed each other's regret.

The music was suddenly just noise. The sofa was suddenly too small for two people. The whole house was too tiny to accommodate Myron and me.

I stood up. You can't really continue to stay seated in this particular variant of an emergency.

He stood up too and went back to his chopping board and his perfectly stimulated lachrymal glands.

I kept standing, not knowing what to do. I let our words hover and settle deep into the red kilim where they could be ignored. But the room had turned to ice.

Myron continued chopping, wiping his eyes with his sleeve.

I should have seen this coming.

So different from the man I met on the eighth of September, the feast of The Assumption, at the SAACA event.

Something, some filament of obligation or kindness flickered within me and compelled me to go to him one more time, even though he had now become an iceberg floating on a distant sea. I walked over to his onion prep, my final gesture of, yes, reparation. The skins were scattered across the counter-top, staining them like a Mandovi sunset. I gathered them all up into a plate.

Finally, 'Bye Bye Blackbird' was filling the room with its sweet-and-sour swing.

'Compost?' I asked.

He looked at me and rose up slightly. He seemed to clutch at a hopefulness in my voice that really wasn't there.

'Can you put onion skins into compost?'

'Yes,' I said, 'you can't put them in a worm farm, the worms don't like them, too acidic. But fine for compost.'

'Fine for compost?'

'Yeah. Add some grass clippings to them next time you do your lawn.'

'I'll save some for you, for the vegetable pigments you were talking about.'

'Onion skins would be interesting.'

'For your *Black Jesus* body of work?'

'For the wounds.'

'I would have thought eggplant skins, no? A deeper purple. Considering he was on the cross for hours?'

On his CD player, the cymbals embellished a piano solo with the lightest of touches.

'Actually the ancient Romans made the colour purple by boiling a large vat of snails.'

'Tyrian purple.'

'Yes.'

'I have plenty of snails in my garden. I could collect them for you. Give them to you.'

The iceberg had begun to reveal itself further. I let him keep speaking.

'Give them to you the next time you come over.'

Then my phone rang. I had left it on the kitchen counter when I first arrived. We could both see it was one of my children calling. The role of chance and children can never be underestimated as an exit strategy.

I reassured Om and Akshar. It was really nothing. I promised I would be home soon.

I disconnected from my children and picked up my handbag in this quickly tropicalising space. We stood facing each other. But we were on different sides of a chasm, now too wide to cross without casualty, his face going under, just as Miles was signing off: *Blackbird bye bye.*

That was yesterday. The night was futile with text messages unsent and unreceived. Here I am today. I am still in my car. His house is solid across the street. His light is on. I can see him now, shadowy, disappearing into a different room. Perhaps he's waiting for me. But this rain will not abate. This rain is a vale of someone else's tears, not mine. This rain is a mask for Myron, not for me. I start up the car. It sounds smooth and dependable. It is dark but the primary colours are clear to me, the primary music is sweet with absolution. The windscreen wipers sharpen the path ahead into a reassuring focus, moving to a beat I won't miss, a metronome for the new pace at which my world will now turn.

Sheela Jaywant has lived all over India as a military nomad in the desert, near the mountains, criss-crossing the continent, eating all sorts of food in all kinds of weather, and collecting stories along the way. She is a humour columnist, travel-writer and some of her stories have won international prizes. Widely anthologised, her single-author anthologies include, *Quilted: Stories of Middle-class India* (2003) and *The Liftman and Other Stories* (2009). The collections in which her work appears are *Carnival, She Writes, Vanilla Desires, Indian Voices, Shell Windows* and *Inside Out*, among others. She translates from Marathi to English. She lives in Sangolda, Goa, and works as a school administrator.

Kokum

SHEELA JAYWANT

Botanists call the tree *Garcinia indica.*

In Maharashtra the fruit is called *kokum,* by which name it is now sold in health-conscious stores, to make 'a refreshing organic drink.' When coconut-milk is added to the extract and seasoned with mustard seeds and curry-leaves, or garlic-paste, it becomes *soal-kadhi,* which is had with steamed rice and fried fish. At crowded, tarpaulin-roofed tin-sheds near petrol-pumps, the highly sweetened, syrupy liquid extract is sold in half-litre plastic jerry-cans. The labels suggest that a diluted version of its contents can 'naturally' cure indigestion, infertility, baldness, cancer, paralysis …

Vijaya, who speaks only Konkani, calls the fruit *birndam soallam* (pronounced bir-hin-dam sohw-lam where the 'm' at the end of both words is silent. It indicates the nasal sound to the preceding syllables). The short-form of the fresh fruit is *birndam.* The short-form of the sun-dried version is *soallam.*

Vijaya sells the *soallam* by the roadside in the months of May and June at the Friday Market and at the *Purmentam-che-Fest* or the pre-monsoon, annual bazaar at Mapusa.

Vijaya sources *birndam* from the hillocks that run parallel to the Chogm Road in Sangolda, a small village in between Porvorim and Saligao, about 6 kms from the tourist infested Calangute-Candolim beach-belt. Few know that Chogm stands for Commonwealth Heads of Government Meeting. The narrow road that was built in 1984 to link the airport via Panaji to the Taj, where the heads of state stayed, is now broad, lined with fancy shops, and accident-prone. Family after family in the neighbourhoods of Porvorim, Pilerne and Saligao have sold ancestral homes, mango-orchards and rice-fields to builders. Estate agents have earned as much in commission on a single deal as their parents made in a lifetime. *Bhaille* or non-Goans from outside the State outnumber the locals here; the local language is pidgin-Hindi, not Konkani.

Vijaya isn't bothered about those things.

'They've cut so many of the tall *brindam* trees in the jungle on the hill,' she tells her invalid husband. 'Where will I get the fruit from?'

She voices another worry: 'Our boys are finding it difficult to repay the loans they've taken to buy taxis. I'm afraid we will sink from being poor to being very poor.'

Her daughters-in-law have jobs in local shops as sales-girls. They keep the *choola* burning. There are squabbles, fisticuffs even, in the mud-walled, two-room hut that they live in, over medicine bills; sometimes, even over the kind of fish bought. (He thinks he's a *baman?* He bought four *bangde* for a hundred rupees; he could have bargained or got ten *tarle* instead.)

Once, Vijaya's eldest son beat her up because she wouldn't part with the small bundle of rupees she had on her. The others intervened; the son and his family walked out, vowing never to return.

She was relieved: 'Fewer mouths to feed.'

So far, the family has kept starvation at bay, worn new clothes at *Chavat,* the Ganapati festival, and bought school-uniforms and text-books for their children.

She persuades her 11-year-old grandson, Mayank, to accompany her into the jungle up the slope. It takes them a couple of false starts and ten minutes to cross through the unending traffic on Chogm Road. There are no pavements. The road's edges fall steeply to the sides and are covered with loose gravel. Vijaya and Mayank walk through the shrubs carrying six black, crumpled but sturdy polythene bags and a long wooden stick, keeping their eyes down to watch out for human faeces along the way. The workers from Bihar, Orissa, Uttar-Pradesh, Jharkhand, Karnataka and the states from the North East, who rent rooms without toilets in Sangolda, are compelled to use this forested area to answer nature's call. Women like Vijaya too relieve themselves in the fields, under cover of darkness, for their homes don't have toilets. On holiday mornings, there are open-air 'community bowel-moving-get-togethers,' where men exchange news.

By eight, Vijaya and Mayank reach the ridge. It's hot and humid; the two share a small bottle of a soft-drink they had bought on the way for 10 rupees, from the little tin-shed shop opposite the panchayat. They take two small sips each, saving the rest for later.

'Even four years ago,' she tells him, 'I could fetch six bucketfuls a day of the plucked fruit. Last year, I got just one bucket.'

She looks around and points to a conical tree about three storeys high. Hundreds of crimson fruit dangle from its branches like baubles on a Christmas tree. She helps Mayank to climb up. Once he's gone as high as he can, she hands him the stick. He stands resting against the trunk, his feet firm on an angular joint. He hits the branches hard with the stick.

'Hit harder,' Vijaya coaxes him. 'Climb higher.'

Encouraged, Mayank climbs a few feet more. He wriggles and flays the stick in all directions. Suddenly, he drops the stick and yells.

'Ants?' Vijaya asks.

'Ai-ai-ai,' he squeals.

'Why didn't you rub the ash before you climbed? Rub it now.'

He balances himself, wraps an arm around a branch, all the while jerking his feet, rubbing the toes of one leg on the calves of the other to get rid of the ants crawling up his bare legs. With the free hand, he takes out of his shirt pocket a paper packet. It contains wood-ash which he rubs over himself. He lowers himself a little and bends to reach out for the stick Vijaya hands him.

For a couple of minutes, he hits the branches as much and as hard as he can. A shower of leaves, twigs and fruit litter the ground.

Most of the fallen fruit are ripe and red, a few still hard and green. Descending, he scrapes a bare thigh and groans.

'Don't fuss,' Vijaya tells him. 'A little bit of hurt harms no one.'

Mayank whimpers and vows never to come with her again.

'None of my friends do this. I won't do it.' He shouts as he jumps to the ground, scratching his body wherever it's itching.

She offers him another sip of the aerated drink and a banana that she's brought along. Caressing his head and running her fingernails over the insect bites on his body, she tells him how brave he is, how precious, how useful to her in her old age.

'*Put,*' she calls him, '*apurbayecho put mozo* (my precious little boy), you will grow big and strong doing this work.'

Mayank is not convinced, but he enjoys her tender strokes on his back.

For a few minutes, the two stand in the shade, enjoying the breeze; silent.

'Get up,' says Vijaya, opening one of the plastic bags, 'we must hurry, otherwise we'll be late for lunch.'

They gather the fallen fruit, discarding those chewed by bats and civet cats, and infested with maggots. They segregate mature ones from the raw, big from small and accordingly put them into different bags. Then, carefully tying the bags at the mouth, around the middle and lengthwise, they stack them on their heads and make their way back home.

The next harvest will be after a year; if the trees aren't cut, that is.

'Wash your hands and feet,' she tells him, 'before entering the house.'

They spread a newspaper on the floor and sit on it; dented steel *taats* before them.

They are served by Mayank's mother. Rice, ground-coconut curry, boiled *bhaji* and a piece of salty, dried fish. After the meal, they rest for a while; then, the entire family gets ready to work on the *birndams*.

In the common space outside their front-door, they sit on their haunches in a loose circle. Neighbours, who share the same open space, come to watch, help or chat. Vijay and her daughters-in-law deftly remove the hilum, break the outer skin and thumb out the flesh within. The peels are broken into small bits and kept in a bucket. The blood-red liquid-flesh — *aagull* — is dumped in a flat wooden vessel. By the time they finish, it is time to put the chickens in the coop and cook dinner: rice-gruel, coconut-curry and spicy chutney on the side.

Next morning, a little after dawn, everyone pitches in to spread the *birndam sollam* on plastic sheets. By evening, under the merciless May sun, the fruits shrivel to half their size. The *aagull* in the wooden vessels is hand-crushed and kept to evaporate. The seeds, with the *aagull* squeezed out of the fibres, to which they are still attached, are spread out to dry on another plastic sheet. From the seeds, sold at ten rupees a kilo, oil will be extracted. This oil is solid at normal temperature and has medicinal properties.

Another day of sunning, and the peels are dried crisp. Then they are rolled in the now-viscous *aagull* and dried again. This dipping-soaking-drying is repeated over three days. The *brindam sollam* are cooled and packed in small plastic pouches, ready to be sold. The pouches are stored in a large sack.

On a hot Friday morning, Vijaya and Mayank lug the sack to the bus-stop. The first bus arrives at seven. Mayank helps her load the sack on to it. Vijaya spends the day sitting on a plastic sheet spread on a pavement, outside one of the shops near the Mapusa bus-stand, between two Gujarati-tribal women who are selling beaded jewellery.

She endures the day on very sweet tea brought in small glasses by urchins who, she believes, steal a packet or two if she's not alert. If she leaves her place for a few minutes, to answer nature's call, someone will occupy it. So she doesn't.

By afternoon, she has sold more than half her stock at 500 per kilo, and made about 2,000 rupees. She must sell the remaining two kilos; can't afford to spend another day and more bus fare on the same harvest.

The afternoon is a lull. Around four, a woman comes by looking for 'cockem' and is guided to Vijaya. She's wearing knee-length pants, a flowery-print blouse, dark glasses and a wide-rimmed hat. Her earrings, fair skin, demeanour and language indicate that she's not Goan. Her companion is just like her.

'Yey cockem hai?' she asks Vijaya.

'Hai, bhai,' Vijaya gives her staccato replies.

'Kitne ka?'

'Paanchshi kilo-chey.'

'500? That's too much, *yaar,'* the companion says.

'Doh-soh mein de doh.' (Make that 200.)

Vijaya is puzzled. Two hundred for all that effort? This money must last her till she can earn from the vegetables planted in the field, harvested at the end of the monsoons in September.

'Nah, bhai,' she says firmly.

Says the woman to her companion: 'They were so humble, so nice when we came here from Delhi two years ago. I could buy the stuff for half of what she's quoting. Now she's not willing to budge. It's gone to their heads, I tell you, this tourism and all ...'

Their conversation veers towards how the prices have gone up in Goa: of food, land, houses, everything. 'But, you know, it was worthwhile shifting here to a nice gated-colony. The fish, the local *bhendi,* the clear air, the slow pace, so-o good for the health.'

They turn to bargain once more.

Meanwhile, Vijaya has sold the lot to someone else. She gathers her plastic sheet and bags, tucks the money into her blouse and goes home satisfied. The two women, used to getting their way, sulk.

In a few years, *Garcinia indica* won't be available for even five times the current rate. Neither Vijaya nor the other women are aware of this.

Prakash S. Parienkar is a multi-award-winning writer and teaches at the Department of Konkani at Goa University. His awards include the Sarvotkrust Sahitya Puraskar 2008, Padmashree B. B. Borkar Memorial Literary Award 2007, Sahitya Akademi Award 2010 for children's literature, and the Dr Jose Pereira Memorial Award 2015 for his book *Mhadei Kallzantylan*. Parienkar has an extensive body of work in the literary field as the author of six books and several screenplays.

Vidya Pai the translator, stumbled onto the field of translation with the Konkani award at the Katha-British Council Translation Contest in 1993. She was an 'outsider', who lived in Kolkata, West Bengal, and spoke the Konkani dialect used by Mangalorean Hindus. So, comprehending the culture, ethos and idiom of Goan writing in Konkani in the Devanagari script was a herculean task. She has translated six Konkani novels: Pundalik Naik's *Acchev* (The Upheaval, OUP, 2002), Mahabaleshwar Sail's *Kali Ganga* (National Book Trust, 2003), *Havthan* (The Kiln, Konkani Language and Cultural Foundation, Mangalore, 2011), *Aranyakand* (Forest Saga, OUP, 2014), *Yug Sanvar* (Age of Frenzy, Harper Perennial, 2017) and Damodar Mauzo's *Karmelin* (Sahitya Akademi, 2004). *Kaleidoscope* (Popular Prakashan, 2008) is her translation of Ravindra Kelekar's essays, and *Mirage and other stories* (Under the Banyan tree, 2014) is her translation of Damodar Mauzo's *Rumadful*. Vidya Pai has been an active volunteer at Hitaishini, a breast cancer support group that runs breast screening clinics in four cancer hospitals in Kolkata.

Abhayaranya
A Forest Sanctuary

Translated from the Konkani to English

PRAKASH S. PARIENKAR, TRANSLATED BY VIDYA PAI

Avdu tied up the cows in the shed and stepped into the front yard. She dropped the load of firewood on the verandah, shook out her crumpled sari and squatted at the edge of the yard. She had beaten the earth smooth and flattened this patch of land in front of her house just eight days ago, but the hens kept shitting and dirtying the place, so this morning, she had applied a fresh coat of dung paste all over its surface.

It was evening and the cool breeze made the whole area quite cold. Layers of darkness seemed to settle on the wooded hills in the distance and soon the area around the house would be submerged in shadows too. At times like this her little house-in-the-woods became a part of the surrounding darkness and staying there alone was a fearful proposition.

A hen and her brood of chicks were darting about in the yard. Champi, the little bitch, stood by the cowshed with her head turned towards the hills. She was barking without pause like she always did when she caught a whiff of some animal moving about in the forest.

A calf lowed in the shed.

'Forgot to set water for that poor calf ... a curse be on me!' Avdu grumbled as she lumbered painfully to her feet. She picked up a pot of water and made her way to the shed.

The hen and chicks had settled down to roost when Avdu returned with Champi sniffing at the ground and frisking about at her heels. She picked up the large basket in the corner and covered the brood. As she stood there in the yard the shadows seemed to seep through her eyes and permeate her whole being, making her a part of the darkness all around. Why does she seem to merge into the surrounding gloom today? Who does she seek in this cold darkness that has trickled down the forested slope?

It must be something momentous or Avdu would not have been shaken to the core. Avdu is not weak-hearted, this mantle of darkness seeping down from the forest cannot scare her. She has been living in close proximity to these shadows in her solitary forest home for many years now.

How many years is it since she got married? She might not know the exact number of years but she has a fair idea. The jackfruit tree in front of the house, the one by which the hens roost at night, is exactly the same age as her marriage. Her father-in-law planted that jackfruit sapling during the first showers of *Meerg* in the year that she was wed. Her husband planted those four coconut palms in the orchard on one side of their house, the year their daughter Vasanthi was born. And Avdu dug pits in the ground and planted the other coconut saplings after the birth of their son Vasu. Three years had passed since her husband Bhathu died, but there was nothing around the house to mark that tragic event.

She hastily gathered the pile of firewood dumped on the verandah and made her way to the kitchen. Feeling her way around in the darkness, she picked up the matchbox from the hearth and lit a lamp. The small, two-room house that had been immersed in darkness all this while was suddenly filled with light. She set cotton wicks in place in the traditional *lamaan-divo* that was lit before the household gods and the tiny *niranjan* oil lamp. She lit both lamps and carried the *niranjan* to its niche beside the sacred tulsi plant in front of the house. Drawing the end of her sari about her, Avdu stooped low before the holy plant, her palms joined in prayer, staring at the dancing flame, letting the tears course through her eyes.

Avdu had broken down and wept freely only two or three times since the day she entered this house as a young bride. The first time was when a tiger killed a calf in their cowshed. The second occasion was when the police arrested her husband on false charges of cutting down trees in the forest. And, like any other woman, Avdu had wailed and sobbed over her husband's dead body. But the tears that spilled out of her eyes at this twilight hour had a different meaning.

Avdu was going to fetch water from the river that morning when her son called out, 'Avai, wait. I must tell you something.'

'What?'

'Avai, let us leave this house and settle down in Kumthal village.' Avdu stared at her son, quite at a loss for words.

'We can build a house of laterite stone blocks. Dhanu kaka, who lives by the temple, has promised to give us land for the house.'

Avdu couldn't utter a word. Her lips trembled and she seemed dumbstruck as darkness descended before her eyes.

'Avai, why are you so quiet? Say something,' Vasu was scared by his mother's reaction though he knew that she would be upset by what he told her.

'The government is evicting people from all the villages that lie on forest land. Sooner or later we shall have to leave, too. Anyway, why should we live here in the middle of the forest?'

Tears rushed into Avdu's eyes when she heard her son's words. She daubed at her eyes with the edge of her sari as a vein throbbed in her temple and her head seemed to spin. She didn't say a word but her tear-filled eyes spoke on her behalf.

'Why do you weep, Avai? How many years will we live in this forest? Let us leave before the government forces us to go. Kumthal is a large settlement, we shall have neighbours who will help us when we are in need. There is a school, a tarred road and a bus passes through the village every morning and evening.' Vasu tried to explain his point of view but she merely stared at him through teary eyes.

'Avai, say something ...'

'Shall we let these cows fall prey to tigers? Shall the fields where we sow a monsoon crop and get enough grain to fill our bellies, turn fallow? Shall we forsake the orchard that your father tended with such care? Your forefathers were born here and they died here, too. Shall we leave them here and move to someone else's village? Who will light the lamp in the Santeri shrine, once we are gone? Tell me, can we leave all this behind and hope to prosper in Kumthal village?' she shrieked.

'But ... the Forester said ...'

'Think I'm scared of that Forester? The government can evict all the other villagers but I'm not going anywhere. If those government fellows come here I'll chop off each one's legs with this sickle! You can go where you want. I will live in Kadval village and I will die here too.'

Avdu rattled off her thoughts stressing every syllable as though spitting fire with every word. Vasu was taken aback. He hadn't expected his mother to be so stubborn about this. Avdu continued to mutter incoherently as she picked up the water pot and moved towards the river.

Kadval is the last settlement in Goan territory and is almost an hour and a half's trek from Kumthal. But Kadval is a village only in name, today. Some hundred and twenty-five years or so ago there were five houses in this settlement, and the families who lived there belonged to the same clan. One year it was seen that the clumps of bamboo in the forest had flowered and developed fresh new shoots. Everyone was delighted. The shoots could be ground to powder, shaped into *bhakris* and cooked on a griddle. They could stock the shoots and have enough food for six months.

Quite contrary to all their expectations, it was tragedy that struck the forest settlement that year. A strange epidemic raged through their village killing three people in a single household in the span of just seven or eight days. Everyone was terrified. They prayed to goddess Santeri for permission to leave the village and three out of the five families, decided to cross the Ghats in search of a new life. One family chose to set down roots in Kumthal village.

Avdu's husband's ancestor, however, chose to remain in the settlement. 'O goddess Santeri, watch over us!' he prayed. 'This site is blessed by your presence. Grant that we may continue to stay here and worship you in this shrine!'

The settlement at Kadval is surrounded by extensive forests. The Mhadei river flows in the valley to the north, and the gurgling sound of the water can be heard in Avdu's house. In the rainy season, when the river is in spate, Avdu can see the surging waters from her home. There is an extensive meadow that slopes down from the house to the river and large glossy boulders, worn smooth by the swirling current, form a boundary wall within which is a small orchard that belongs to her family. On the western side are fields where crops are grown during the rains. To the south and the east are low hills with cashew groves.

If one walks eastwards from Kadval for an hour or so, one can get to Krishnapur village which is in the state of Karnataka. All these settlements are connected by well-worn mud tracks, one of which passes through the plain just beyond Avdu's house.

Gharu and Ganpat, residents of Krishnapur village, had gone to Goa on some work. As they were returning home that evening they stopped at Avdu's house to rest awhile.

'*Gey Kadval-karni* … I hear your government will evict you from this forest soon,' Gharu said respectfully, hoping to hear something new about the government's proposed Abhayaranya project.

'We'll see. They've been saying that for two or three years, now.'

'The government will pay compensation to those who have valid land documents,' Ganpat declared. 'They'll also give funds for building a new house. You'll get a lot of money for your house and your land.'

Avdu Kadval-*karni* would get a lot of money soon, and she and her son would turn wealthy overnight, Gharu thought. He and Ganpat had crossed Bondir and Kajherjhat villages on the way and everyone was talking about the amount of compensation each evicted family would receive.

'Kadval-*karni,* all this is fine, but we Krishnapur-*kars* will suffer because of this. Your government will seal this area and won't let us use this track.'

'They won't let us take this route to the Valpoi market when we come with loads of cashew in summer,' the men rued. The forest sanctuary project filled them with dismay. They travelled to Goa very often and always used this forest track. If it was sealed off they would have to take the much longer route through Khanapur.

One rarely saw forest guards in this region in the old days, but over the past two years, ever since the forest was declared a protected area or Abhayaranya, the guards are seen making their rounds. The forest department has erected barbed wire fences around the open spaces in the jungle. And during the last rainy season they planted saplings in these enclosed spaces.

It was around the time of the Shigmo festival last year that a jeep stopped on the track one afternoon and the Forester sahib, John Aravjo, came up to Avdu's house. They made small talk for a while and then the sahib asked to see the land documents. Avdu made Vasu climb on to the loft and look through the objects stored in the wooden chest, but Vasu couldn't find any land deed. His father had never shown him any such papers, he thought, as he climbed down from the loft.

'If you cannot produce a land deed to prove ownership this will be deemed forest land in our records and will pass to the government,' Aravjo sahib declared. A sense of fear gnawed at Avdu's heart.

'We have been living in Kadval village for so many years. How can this land belong to the government, then?'

'You have a point. But there must be legal proof that the land belongs to you.'

'We sow the monsoon crop in these fields. We have cashew groves on the hills and an orchard with coconut palms and banana trees. So much yield … how can you say that the land does not belong to us?' she asked.

'We're not bothered about the yield. We need valid documents to prove that you own this land. And even if you produce the land deed, you will have to leave this place.'

'But there is a temple in the middle of the orchard, where can we go leaving our family deity Santeri behind?'

'If you have valid documents the government will pay you for the land. You will get adequate compensation for the house and for the yield that you get from this land. But you cannot go against the decision that has been taken by the government,' the Forester declared.

Avdu's heart quaked and she seemed drained of all physical and mental energy on hearing these words. Her body began to tremble and she didn't have the strength to ask him anything further. Vasu's father had never spoken to him about the land deed, so the youth had no idea whether the document existed at all. The Forester took Vasu down to where the jeep was parked and they spent a long time discussing the matter.

Avdu was unable to sleep that night. She set off early the next morning for her daughter's home in Kodali village and told her son-in-law all that had happened. The young man wasted no time. He came home with Avdu and accompanied Vasu to the panchayat office and then to the Land Revenue Office to see if there were any documents showing that the land had been registered in the family's name. They found no such documents and Avdu seemed to lose all hope.

The villagers of Bondir and Kajherjhat were going to meet the MLA in connection with the Abhayaranya project so Vasu decided to go along too.

'All of you must vacate the area that has been marked as a forest sanctuary,' the elected representative of government declared.

'Those of you who possess valid documents will be paid the cost of the land. The government will give the others a plot of land elsewhere and enough money to build a house. But no one will be allowed to retain land within the Abhayaranya.'

Vasu returned home, disappointed at his words.

Avdu's parents used to live in a little village high up in the Ghats. She was married at the age of thirteen and in those days people would flock to the forest around the Mhadei river to practice *kumer* farming, a form of shifting agriculture. After the new year festival, scores of people carrying knives and sickles and axes would head to these forests to chop down trees and vegetation and set the debris alight. As the first showers of rain fell in *meerg*, *nassaney* grains would be sown in these clearings.

Avdu's husband's family were the *gaunkars,* the earliest settlers in this region, so they had to give permission before anyone could cut down trees within the borders of Kadval village. They performed all the rituals to appease the gods during the agricultural process and once the *nassaney* crop was harvested and threshed, each farmer would offer the family two *kudavs* of grain as a mark of respect.

In later years the government banned this form of shifting cultivation and the number of people who flocked to the forest decreased. Hills that had been laid bare of vegetation were covered with trees again and the thick forest spread on all sides.

The government began the process of surveying the forest land around that time and when the villagers of Kumthal told Avdu's father-in-law about this he was unimpressed. This land belonged to my forefathers. Why should it be surveyed? Who will take it away, he asked, refusing to get the survey done. His family didn't bother to get the land surveyed in later years.

The MLA's statement that they would have to vacate the forest area earmarked for the Abhayaranya kept ringing in Vasu's ears and he couldn't sleep that night. Why should we stay here any longer if we have to vacate our land anyway, he thought. The villagers of Bondir and Kajherjhat will get plots of land somewhere far away. Wouldn't it be better to accept that plot in Kumthal village and build a house there before the government forces us to leave the forest? Thoughts like these kept whirling in his mind these days as he made plans to leave the forest.

When Avdu got back from the river, she couldn't see her son anywhere around. She went down to the orchard and then to the meadow where the cattle grazed.

'Now where did this boy go without telling me anything,' she muttered to herself. This sense of unease increased as the afternoon turned to evening. She had hoped that Vasu, who had left home early that morning, would return by dusk, but things did not turn out that way.

Avdu thought of Vasu as she placed the *niranjan* by the sacred tulsi plant. He was conscious of the fact that after his father's death, his mother was alone in that forest house, so he took care to return home at night. These days he was out for much of the day, but he always returned home before his mother ate her dinner and went to bed.

Champi began to bark and Avdu sensed that people were passing along the forest track. Perhaps Vasu is bringing someone home, she thought for a moment, but the voices disappeared in the forest.

She lit a fire in the hearth and set the water to boil, tossing enough rice into the pot for herself and Vasu as well. She rushed out to the verandah when she heard the slightest noise, but Vasu did not come. Avdu ate her dinner and lay down in bed. Now where had this boy gone? Who could have put this thought of moving to Kumthal into his head? Wretched people must have told my boy some tall stories ... and this foolish fellow believed them! We own all this land here, why should we go and stay in someone else's village?

As the Forester sahib's image flashed before her eyes she remembered the dispute they had had that day. She bristled with anger. Something must be done about these forest officials! Let them come here again, I'll strip each one naked and drive him out of sight!

Avdu awoke at daybreak and milked the cows. She drank some tea, let the cows loose so that they could graze in the meadow and set off for Kumthal. She asked everyone she met if they had seen Vasu and soon the whole village was abuzz with the news that Vasu was missing and his mother, the Kadvalkarni was looking for him. No one in these forest areas knew her as Avdu. She was always referred to, with respect, as 'the Kadvalkarni,' the venerable lady from Kadval village.

When she got home she saw her daughter Vasanthi sitting on the verandah.

'Where did you go, Avai, I've been waiting for such a long time.'

'Vasu is missing since yesterday. Who knows where the boy has gone.'

'He is in my house. He came yesterday.'

'Left his mother here all alone and set off for your house? I've been looking for him in Kumthal since this morning.' Avdu was furious.

'Why are you so worried, where will he go leaving you here all alone?

'He says he doesn't want to live in the forest.'

'He told me about that. And also that he wants to get married,' Vasanthi explained.

'Have I stopped him from getting married?'

'Which girl will agree to marry him and live in this forest, Avai? He's not getting any younger now.'

'Why? Didn't I get married to your father? What was there in the forest in those days? No neighbours, no friends. All the relatives had already fled from the village by then.'

'But will today's girls agree to live in the forest?'

'Don't worry about Vasu, he's just being stubborn. I'll reason with him. And if he agrees, I'll look for a suitable bride and get him married, too,' Vasanthi assured her mother as she set off home the next morning.

Four days passed in this manner. On the fifth morning at about ten, a jeep stopped on the forest track and four officials from the Forest Department came to Avdu's house.

'Kadvalkarni the government has sent you a notice. You must vacate this place before the rains start in Meerg,' the Forester sahib said. Avdu realized that this was not the same official who had come to her house the last time.

'Yesterday we distributed notices in Bondir village and Kajherjhat. Today we have come to see you,' the official said, handing Avdu a notice and pressing her ink-smeared thumb on a sheet of paper.

'Say something, now. You were very vocal last time, when Aravjo sahib was here, why are you quiet now?' one of the guards who had come the last time, raised his voice threateningly.

'There will be a meeting at your panchayat office on the tenth of next month, that is twenty days from now,' the Forester said. 'The minister, the MLA, the collector, the revenue officer of your *taluka* and the sarpanch will be there. The government will allot plots of land at Gomalla on that day, and those of you who do not have land ownership papers will also get financial help. But you must not stay at home and send your son. If he goes alone, when you are still alive, your family will get nothing. You will have to be present there, do you understand?' the Forester asked.

Avdu nodded silently and the group set off, talking amongst themselves. Avdu stared after them till they vanished in the distance.

Nine days had passed since Vasanthi had come home. No one came to Avdu's house after that and she began to lose hope that Vasu, who had left home in a fit of anger, would ever come back.

✳

The sun was setting and Avdu's cows were grazing by the compound wall in the meadow as they did every evening. Suddenly, the noise of crackers bursting near the Santeri temple in the orchard, agitated the cattle. Tambu the cow who was grazing by the wall, raised her tail and rushed towards the shed. The little calf that was grazing by her side raised its ears in alarm and followed on her heels. Champi, who had been sprawled in the yard, rushed towards the orchard barking loudly and the hens, that had settled down to roost began clucking in alarm.

The small group of people that had emerged from the temple moved towards Avdu's house and stepped into the yard. The door of the house was wide open so Vasanthi called out to her mother, 'Avai, come out! See, Vasu is here!'

When there was no response, Vasanthi stepped into the house while Vasu and his bride stood in the yard with their eyes trained on the door. What will my mother say when she hears that I'm married? Will she be furious or will she be delighted to see her daughter-in-law?

'Babu, Avai isn't in the house. Where could she go at this twilight hour?' Vasanthi rushed out nervously.

'Must be somewhere around. She hasn't tied up the cows in the shed. Why would she go anywhere leaving the house open like this?' Vasanthi's husband tried to reassure his wife.

Vasu didn't waste any more time.

'Bhavoji, go and check by the river. I'll cut across to the fields and see if she is there.'

As the others stood in the yard waiting for Vasu to return, Vasanthi went in and out of the house restlessly. She saw the ladder resting against the entrance to the loft and wondered if her mother could have seen them coming and chosen to hide up there. She climbed the ladder and peeked into the loft but there was no one there. She went out into the yard and looked up at the branches of the trees around the house.

'Avai isn't in the fields,' Vasu said as he rushed back home trying to catch his breath. Vasanthi's husband returned in a short while.

'She isn't by the river, either. I looked around in the orchard, didn't see her anywhere.'

'Avai must be somewhere close by. Finish the rituals quickly and let the bride and groom enter the house,' Vasanthi's husband suggested.

Vasanthi went inside, wiping her eyes. She soon emerged with a tumbler of water, a lighted lamp and some *haldi* and *kumkum* on a tray. Vasu and his bride stood on the threshold as Vasanthi sprinkled water on their feet. She smeared some turmeric and vermilion on their foreheads, waved the flickering lamp about their faces, and escorted the bride into the house.

'Let us go right now and see if she is in Kumthal village,' Vasu declared as he changed his clothes, and tucked his scythe into the belt at his waist.

He slipped a matchbox into his pocket and picked up a torch. They set off at a brisk pace stopping awhile at Bondir and Kajherjhat to check if anyone had seen Avdu, but when they received no favourable response they moved on to his uncle's house in Kumthal. Dhanu was sorry to hear that the old lady who had been scouring the area looking for her son just the other day, was nowhere to be seen.

It was around ten that night when they returned home. Vasanthi broke down on hearing that her mother was nowhere to be found, but Dhanu kaka's presence seemed to calm her down.

'Where can we look for her in the middle of the night? We will go to Krishnapur tomorrow and if she is not there we can go to Gavali, where her parents lived in the old days,' he said.

Vasu and Dhanu kaka set off early the next morning for Krishnapur and visited the few houses in the village, speaking to the elderly villagers. They reached Gavali village that afternoon but when Vasu realized that no one had news of Avdu, he was totally dejected and filled with guilt.

It's because of me that my mother chose to leave home, he said to himself. Why did I get angry with her? Why did I leave home without informing her? Bhavoji fixed up my marriage with his sister Shakuntala. I am a married man now, I am not alone. My wife Shakuntala has visited our home in Kadval village many times. She knows everything about this place, yet she agreed to this marriage. She must be very upset that her mother-in-law has left home.

It was late in the evening when they got home to Kadval village. Vasu went down to the river and sat on a rock staring at the water. The sun had set and darkness was settling on the land as the Mhadei gurgled and surged past the rocks.

The picture of Shakuntala, sitting silently in the house swam up before Vasu's eyes. His sister and brother-in-law and uncle would return to their homes. Then Shakuntala and he would be the only ones in the forest. His mother did not want to leave Kadval village, she had made up her mind to live in the forest. So she must be somewhere in the forest, true to her word.

The government will evict all those villagers who live within the limits of the Abhayaranya, so we will have to leave this place. But how can I let Avai wander in the forest while I move away?

It was getting very dark as Vasu got up and moved homewards. The house was immersed in the surrounding darkness and insects buzzed noisily all around. As Vasu trudged home on leaden feet he noticed two people making their way down the forest track; their voices carried to his ears.

'That Kadvalkarni's son isn't quite right in the head. If he were all right, she would not have left home,' one man said.

'Must have killed herself.'

'She wouldn't do that. Must be wandering about in the forest.'

The news that the Kadvalkarni was nowhere to be seen had spread throughout the forest settlements. Some people said that Avdu Kadvalkarni had killed herself in a fit of rage against her son. Some people thought that she had turned mad and was roaming about in the forest at the top of the Ghats. Others said that her son had killed her because he wanted the money that the government would pay the evicted villagers. Yet another group of people claimed that she was hiding in the forest, waiting to kill the Forest officials.

Who knows who is right and who is wrong? Who, but the spirit of the Abhayaranya, can answer these questions?

Glossary

Lamaan-divo	Devotional hanging lamp.
Meerg	Light showers of rain.
Avai	Mother.
Kaka	Uncle.
Bhavoji	Brother-in-law.
Bhakri	Flat bread baked on a griddle.
Ghats	A range of mountains along Goa's eastern flank.
Gey	A respectful honorific used when addressing an older woman.
Kadval-karni	A lady who hails from Kadval village.
Krishnapur-kar	A man who hails from Krishnapur.
Shigmo	A Goan festival marking the advent of Spring.
Nassaney	A cereal.
Kudav	A measure for solids.

Steve R. E. Pereira is a Goan Tanzanian/Canadian/Australian queer-identified artist and activist. A theatre graduate, Steve is particularly proud of having worked at Theatre Fountainhead (Toronto's first black theatre company, now defunct) and for producing and directing *It's a Goan Thing* an ensemble production exploring the particular in-betweenness of being a Canadian Goan, in celebration of the Toronto Goan Overseas Association's 25th Anniversary. In Toronto, Steve was the founding member of Desh Pardesh, an arts service organisation and as the artistic director helped develop an annual multi-disciplinary arts festival that became one of the largest South Asian arts festivals in North America. Steve also worked as a programmer and curator for the Inside/Out Film Festival and on the editorial board of *Fuse* magazine. He has been published in *Fuse, Borderline, ATOM, Toronto Star, Joao Roque Literary Journal* and *Bent St.,* an anthology of queer Australian writing. In Melbourne, Australia, where he currently lives, Steve most recently adapted, produced and directed Ugandan writer Okot p'Bitek's epic poems *Song of Lawino* and *Song of Ocol* into a theatrical performance called *The Graceful Giraffe Cannot Become a Monkey* for the Big West Festival. Steve is the founder and director of the now annual Sunshine Short Film Festival and the inaugural Brimbank Music of the World Festival.

A Dolphin in the Ganges

Steve R. E. Pereira

The first two things that Raymund bought after his father and mother ceremoniously presented him with the tickets at his graduation party were bathing trunks in glittering gunmetal and a pair of sunglasses. The trunks were Armani, the glasses not made by anybody worth mentioning. But he had so admired them on Paul. It made him feel better not just because he did look particularly buff in the swimsuit, but because he knew his father would not approve. And he wanted to get him back. He had specifically asked for a trip to Paris. And what did he get? Bloody Goa. Bloody family.

Then the frenzied days of squabbling over his blond tips (What will people think?), inoculation-taking, money-changing, squabbling over his three silver-stud earrings (Why do you have to make such a spectacle of yourself?), present-shopping, squabbling over his nose-ring (Do you not have any shame?), packing, packing, squabbling over the clothes he was packing (What will people say?), novena-saying, unpacking, repacking …

Throughout it all, he'd quelled his growing irritation with visions of himself buffed and bronzed, stretched out on the golden sand, beneath swaying coconut trees, the ocean a swathe of shimmering blue sparkling in the foreground. And hovering around the peripheries of his postcard-perfect picture — this he realized in their startling absence after he got there — were the other expectations of 'exotic' travel: a five-star hotel with acres of cool marble, solicitous uniformed staff, and sleek, tanned bodies littered around a series of impossibly aquamarine pools. That was what he'd expected prior to his arrival. But the homecoming was quite something else.

It was only on the third day after he arrived that Raymund got to go to the beach. It was Sunday, and after the ritual of breakfast at eight, mass at Holy Name of Mary's across the road at ten-thirty, lunch at noon, siesta until two-thirty — only then did they, with much chatter, troop down behind the house, to the beach beyond the sand dunes. It was two minutes away, but it could have been halfway across the state, such an expedition it became. In an unarticulated coda that governed rules of acceptable behaviour. Sunday was, Raymund was able to gather, the one day of the week when it was permissible to go to the beach. Perhaps it had something to do with the balancing influence of mass in the morning. Otherwise, the beach was considered verboten; a hangout for rubbish people, lewd behaviour, drug-crazed hippies, and god-knows-what-else-ness. This he was told on his first morning, when looking around at the 22 versions of his father who had arrived to meet him for the first time. They were now looking back at him with just as much horror as he was looking at them when he asked about the beach.

After a week of being ferried around to innumerable, insufferably inquiring and disapproving relatives, Raymund began to affect an escape by announcing rather grandly that he had decided he would like to do a tour of India. To see, he said, the Taj Mahal, the temples, the museums and things like that. 'After all, I am here all the way from Melbourne,' and he sighed as he said this, hoping to ingratiate himself by invoking a certain amount of pious responsibility. 'And who knows when I will be able to come back again. I may as well do some travelling now, see the rest of India.'

The truth was that he had a limited idea of what he wanted to see in India. His trip to Goa was a reluctant concession to parental pressure. There was an obligation here to renew ancestral ties strained by the exigencies of what his grandfather considered exile — his father's migration — and what he regarded as good fortune, especially after meeting his extended family. Saccharin memorialising had attempted to bridge the gulf between places and generations but here, now, aside from a litany of family names, he knew little of the place, and frankly, cared much less. His mistake was that, in his anticipation of a month on a tropical beach, he hadn't quite prepared for the smothering attention accorded a prodigal return. He had to get away; the questions were becoming progressively more awkward and personal.

His uncle was not convinced about the proposed travel. He fixed Raymund with his rheumy eye and in a sputtering of gestures and fatuous profanity — this bloody, bloody that — he painted the world outside Goa — no — actually, the world outside the tennis club, the family compound, and the Church, in that order, as a tangle of primitive, heathen, dark, hostile forces. Here, the uncle who was given to pompous announcements, announced very pompously: 'Here is FAMILY. Here is five hundred years of Portuguese rule/church/civilisation. Here was once the Pearl of the Orient.'

The uncle paused and wagged a finger in Raymund's face.

'Do you know why we are known as the Irish of India?' he asked.

Raymund did not.

'We are the Irish of India because we too love the whisky and the music.' The uncle was positively triumphant. There was nothing to say to that.

Raymund was saved eventually by a no-nonsense senior aunt visiting from Bombay who decided on things by saying that she couldn't see that it would do him any harm, and with one of her unsettling looks said that he was far too Australian for his own good anyway. And that pretty much settled that.

Taking him in tow back with her to Bombay, the somewhat terrifying aunt took charge. She snipped the blond tips off herself and stripped Raymund of his earrings, nose ring, and layers of attitude with a brisk, 'We don't tolerate that nonsense here.' Perched in her tiny cramped apartment in teeming Bandra and armed with his contribution to the exercise — a *Lonely Planet* guide purchased at the bookshop of the Taj Mahal Hotel — they mapped out a much-subdued Raymund's passage through India. Well, northern India anyway. Bombay to Varanasi to Delhi to Agra to Jaipur to Udaipur then across to Calcutta, then up to Kathmandu; pitstops in a positively dizzying array of places. That was the plan. As it turned out, Raymund never made it past his first stop, Varanasi.

The flight from Bombay to Varanasi was fine, the hostel a tad too rustic for Raymund's taste, but also fine. The contretemps began the morning after his arrival.

In the grey-silver crispness of a Varanasi morning, Raymund negotiated his way down the silted-up steps of the ghat to the river-edge. Further downstream, the bustle had already begun along the bank; pilgrims lined up for the first of their immersions in the holy river while priests, flower-sellers and beggars readied for the business of religion. Further up the river, at some of the accessible ghats, he looked enviously at the vanloads of chattering tourists being gingerly assisted into canopied boats for the obligatory dawn river excursion.

Raymund was on his own. He had negotiated the previous night with a boatman recommended by the proprietor of the hostel. Fifty rupees for one hour on the river beginning at five in the morning — a bargain, he was told, for a private expedition. He didn't much care for the privacy; he would have preferred to share with other tourists, not just for the economy of it but for the inconspicuousness it would have afforded. He could deal with being an object of curiosity for western tourists, he was used to being exotic in Melbourne. But Raymund had arrived too late to join a group excursion, and he only really had a day in the city.

He was to meet the boatman at four-thirty. It was four-forty. A boat was pulled up by the concrete mooring on the river, not the gaily canopied vessel that had been there yesterday, but a smaller, much more dilapidated one sans colour, sans canopy. Yesterday's boat and boatman were nowhere in sight.

Raymund perched on the prow of the boat, his back to the river as he scanned the banks for the errant boatman. He had paid a deposit, not much, but still. Where the hell was the boatman? His uncle was right. They were all thieves. Bloody, bloody, bloody hell. Raymund didn't want his uncle to be right about anything. He jiggled his legs in frustration. He didn't realise he was making the vessel rock until the yelled oath — *'Arre sala!'* — from the depths, startled Raymund into leaping away from the boat. Unfortunately, the incline of the bank made him trip over his feet and brought him to his knees.

Fighting off the pain, Raymund looked around. There was a man standing up in the boat lighting a kerosene lantern. This definitely was not the boatman from the previous night. Beautiful god. The gnat of a thought pinged across Raymund's mind. The man … boy … man/boy looked down at him. Raymund thought there was something boyish about him, even though they could have been the same age. A grin, a very sexy one, slowly crept across the billowy curves of the boatman/boy's lips.

'You boat ride?' the god-face asked.

Raymund was disconcerted and stared blankly. The boy lifted his chin at Raymund and winked. Raymund realised that he wasn't perhaps in the most dignified position; on his hands and knees looking over his ass at the man. Well, not the best position in which to be holding a conversation.

'My uncle. You made business with my uncle,' said the boy.

Raymund stood up hurriedly, dusting off his palms and knees. He was a little disconcerted. This wasn't what he expected, not at all. He must be cold, he thought — those shorts are very thin. So very thin.

'Where is your uncle?' he asked, trying to sound stern and regain some dignity. The boy's grin was too knowing, too close to a leer for Raymund's liking.

'My agreement was with your uncle. Where is he?'

He tried to sound as stern and as Aussie as he could. He needed to control this situation.

'He other people,' was the response as the boy gestured vaguely up the river. 'No problem, I take you.'

The boat was in the water now, and the boy was holding it steady at the pier waiting for him to climb in. 'Come, sir. No problem. I am good. You like me.'

Troubled by the 'sir' and deciding to ignore the even more unsettling 'you like me', Raymund walked to the edge of the pier to where the boy was with the boat. The drop down was steeper than Raymund had expected. He stood at the edge, looking down uncertainly at the boy. Then suddenly, with a laugh, the boy wrapped both arms around Raymund's upper thighs and lifted him cleanly off the pier. Swivelling, he slid Raymund down his body, and set him down in the boat. They stood there for a beat, the boy laughing down at Raymund's burning face while Raymund tried hard not to be conscious of the point of pressure from the boy against the front of his hip. It wasn't the boy's hand. Then a swell from a passing motorboat conveniently sent Raymund stumbling back, and he fell onto the seat. The boy chuckled as he stepped around to the till. Raymund absorbed himself in setting up his camera.

Unsettled even before the expedition had begun, Raymund didn't hear most of what the boy tried to tell him about the schedule of the expedition as he navigated the boat away from the pier and into the river. He was grateful he had his back to the boy and just nodded when it seemed a nod was called for. He was uneasily conscious of the boy's curiosity in him. But he put a quick damper on his interest when the boy asked, 'You are from India?'

His look back was glacial as he said, 'No, Australia. I told your uncle yesterday.' He wasn't encouraging any more impertinence.

A little later, as they negotiated past other boatloads of tourists, he saw the uncle, the man he had talked to the day before, rowing a packed load of tourists who were busy chatting. The uncle waved at him enthusiastically as the boats paralleled one another. Shouting across the chasm of the river between them, he pointed to his boatload: 'Australian also.' Snouts of video cameras locked onto him as bacon-red faces looked up at the boatman blankly then turned to look at him curiously. He didn't offer a greeting, and the boats soon swept past each other. The boy snickered behind him. Raymund turned around. He had forgotten — how could he forget — how good-looking the boy was.

The boy winked at Raymund. 'You Australian, ya?'

The upping and downing of the eyebrows combined with the grin was confusing. Raymund couldn't figure out if the boy was making fun of him.

He decided he had had enough. Besides, now he could see more clearly what was in the river and it wasn't attractive. No matter what the boy said, Raymund couldn't believe that dolphins or any other fish could survive in the effluence that was the river. He said to the boy, 'Enough. I want to go back.'

The boy looked surprised and said, 'Still twenty minutes.'

Raymund didn't know how he could know that, since he didn't have a watch on but didn't want to get into it.

'Never mind, I will give you the full payment. Go back now.'

The boy's lips gave a quick twitch, but he said, 'OK. You boss,' and turned the boat around.

'Fifty rupees, your uncle agreed,' Raymund said, when he was standing on the bank. 'Fifty rupees for two hours.'

'OK ...' said the boy, adding a breath too late and with a smirk that belied any sincerity, ' ... *saab.'* Raymund avoided looking at the boy, added another 20 rupees as a tip, said thank you very politely, and climbed up the sides of the embankment as fast as he could.

It was hot, humid, and the throng were already bustling at the banks of the river. Walking carefully around the huge sheets drying on the steps, he went into his hostel. He had a shower, sought relief from a throbbing erection in the sputtering stream of cold water, and felt better for it. Even so, the knowing grin of the boy lingered on in his mind as he lay sweltering on his bed. After an hour of futile rest, he went out again. It was already too hot to do any walking so he, for the first time grateful for the inconspicuousness of being able to blend into the crowds, sat on the steps of the nearest ghat and pretended to be absorbed in a book.

He was caught out almost at once. A muscular South Indian-looking man emerged dripping from the river, and locked gaze with Raymund as he stepped up the incline. Raymund held his look for a second, but then lost courage and looked away. When he chanced a look back, the man who was adjusting his wet *lungi,* let it slip open revealing an impressive thatch of dark, wiry hair and a thick, hooded dark root between his legs.

Raymund played it cool. He looked at the man's crotch until it was covered up again, raised his eyes to meet the man's, then deliberately looked away to the river and then back to pretend-reading his book. He didn't look up as he heard the man go past him, particularly when he heard the man mutter angrily to the back of his head, *'Apni gaand mein muthi daal.'* (Put your fist up your ass.)

His attention was caught though when there was an unexpected loud and guttural rejoinder from a familiar voice. *'Arre, chutia, kya baat hai?'* (You fucker what's the matter?)

That reduced all the chatter around them to silence. Raymund looked up. It was the boy from the boat facing off against the South Indian man. A space had instantly cleared between them. The crowd, as always, were spoiling for a fight. There was a beat of silence, then the South Indian man sucked his teeth noisily at the boy and jerked his head in Raymund's direction.

'Kya yeh aapkee kutiya hai?' (Is this your bitch?), he asked contemptuously. Immediately, attention switched to Raymund and an excited buzz began to circulate.

Raymund was feeling sick. His face was on fire but there was a ball of ice where his stomach was. He turned to get away but immediately two men on either side of him grabbed his arms and held him in place. Their grip hurt. One of the men put his face right up to Raymund's and snarled, *'Tum kahan ja rahe ho, kutiya?'* (Where are you going, bitch?)

Raymund recoiled as much from the aggression as from the sour smell that came off the man. He was more frightened than he had ever been in his life. He knew enough about mob violence in India to be properly terrified. He squeezed his eyes shut. Involuntarily a prayer bubbled from his lips, 'Hailmaryfullofgrace.'

Deep breath. 'Holymarymothergodprayussinnersnowandtilldeathamen.'

He didn't know how many times he repeated the inchoate prayer, how long he was standing there or when or how the yelling and chaos around him ended. But end it did, and Raymund suddenly felt himself being released. He opened his eyes, blinking against the harsh light.

Four policemen were standing at the top of the steps grimly surveying the crowd, slapping their wooden batons against their palms. The two men holding him were gone. So was the crowd which had dissipated as quickly as it had formed. It was the usual bustle and business as though nothing had occurred. The South Indian man had vanished but as Raymund looked around, breathing deeply, there was the boy from the boat. He winked at Raymund, a smile twitching the corners of his mouth.

'Arrey, yaar, Aussie,' (Hey Aussie), the boy said.

He stepped up to Raymund and held out an offering in his hand. It was his camera lens-cap. Raymund had left it on the boat and in his discombobulation, hadn't even noticed the loss.

Raymund wanted nothing more than to not be there, but he didn't want to draw any more attention to himself and that boy was right in front of him. There was no getting away. He had difficulty meeting the boy's knowing eyes, but between the eyes and the too-thin shorts, the eyes were easier to deal with. He took the lens-cap, thanked him, and offered the boy a handful of notes. The boy pushed back Raymund's proffered hand and said, 'No.'

Raymund looked at him in alarm.

The boy looked at Raymund unsmiling. 'Take my picture.'

Raymund just looked at him blankly, so the boy leaned in closer and said more deliberately, 'You. Take. Photo. Me.'

There wasn't a whole lot of choice. Raymund said, 'OK.'

The boy posed in front of him, a Bollywood pose; leaning back, arms folded across his chest, one hand cradling his chin. He looked good. Raymund clicked and clicked again. He didn't see any point in telling the boy that the sun was coming in the wrong way, that the photos would be too dark. He clicked a couple more shots, even turning the camera around horizontally to show that he knew what he was doing. Finally, he lowered the camera and said, 'All right.'

But the boy hadn't had enough.

'Now like Stallone,' he said and took off his t-shirt, hunching his shoulders up in a muscle pose.

Grinning, he segued through a series of poses. A crowd gathered, Raymund was sweating, but the audience was whistling and clapping admiringly. Raymund clicked away, though this time he did move around. The circle of people required a better performance from him. Plus, this way he had an easier escape route to his hostel.

'Hey,' the boy said suddenly. Startled, Raymund lowered his camera and looked at him.

'You think I look like Rambo?'

There was that sly smile again as the boy moved his palms over the muscular planes of his chest, thumbs flicking blackberry nipples in passing. His laugh was coarse and was echoed in the large crowd that had gathered around them. The boy was playing up to the audience.

'You Australian,' he said, 'me Rambo,' and laughed.

There were approving chuckles all around. Raymund felt the blood drain from his face, which then turned very hot. He looked down at the camera, fiddling with it.

'I will send you the pictures,' he said finally.

The boy laughed. He reached out and held up Raymund's chin. The touch was gentle and then it was gone. The boy slipped his t-shirt back on.

'OK,' he said to Raymund and then with a blow of a kiss, he was gone.

Raymund made his way back to the hostel where he barricaded himself in his room that night. The next day he changed his ticket to fly back to Bombay and three days later he was back in Melbourne. He put down his early return to not feeling well. His parents didn't say anything about the new sober-looking, sober-attitude Raymund, and didn't ask any questions about the photos of the bare-chested boy he kept hidden in his sock drawer. For his part, Raymund caught up with Paul and went on with his life. Sort of. At the back of his mind for years after, he just wished he had asked the boy for his name.

Rochelle Potkar is the author of *The Arithmetic of Breasts and Other Stories* (fiction) and *Four Degrees of Separation* (poetry). She is an alumna of Iowa's International Writing Program and the Charles Wallace Writer's Fellowship, Stirling. 'The Leaves of the Deodar' won her the 2016 Open Road Review Contest. Widely anthologised, her story *Chit Mahal* (The Enclave) appears in *The Best of Asian Short Stories* (2017) by Kitaab International and her poem 'The Girl from Lal Bazaar' was shortlisted for the Gregory O' Donoghue International Poetry Prize, 2018. *Paper Asylum* (Copper Coin Publishing, May 2018) is her latest book publication. Most recently, her poem, 'Skirt' has been adapted into a poetry film by Philippa Cousins (UK), for the Visible Poetry Project 2018, USA. Her poem 'War Specials' was runner-up for the pan-India Great Poetry Contest 2018, and 'To Daraza' won the Norton Girault Literary Prize 2018.

The Metamorphosis of Joe Pereira

ROCHELLE POTKAR

Joe Pereira sat in his cane chair every evening as mosquitoes crowded his head.

Buzz buzz.

'Tcha!' with a sweep of his hand.

Children ran screaming round and round in the compound.

'Catch me! Aaah! No!'

'Shut up all of you. Spoilt the peace of my life,' screamed Joe in a quivering voice.

'Get down from that gate,' he said, standing up on his first-floor verandah.

'Swinging on it like it was a swing. I will complain to the secretary.'

His voice went hoarse with phlegm and then mute.

He sat down, only to be provoked this time by coconut gatherers.

'Who asked you to climb the tree? Robbers! Not one coconut left on the tree. Take it to the market and sell it for two-two rupees. Thieves! They're worth much more. Papa had planted them.'

The children's screaming, Joe's screaming and the coconut gatherers' laughter blend to make the evening a pleasant, noisy, happening one — the usual for passers-by and brisk walkers on the street, in front of the old bungalow on West Avenue.

A large resounding tap on the main door, and Joe rushes to answer it as echoes of his footsteps follow him. Mrs Clair would send him subsidised food in a hot case for 200 rupees a month. Joe would eat half of it in the night — curry and bread — and the other half in the afternoon — curry and rice. For breakfast, it was always a *pav* and a cup of tea made with milk powder.

Next, came the *pavwala*. Tap tap.

There was no maid to open the door. Joe had asked her to leave after she had opened the door to sweaty men who came into the house and took furniture and crockery down and out through the basement gate, that stood at the centre of the bungalow like a yawn. The men gave her 50 rupees for fine bone chinaware, 500 rupees for the rosewood curio cupboard, and 1000 rupees for the teakwood wardrobe, a blue oxidized chain lamp and a bottle with a ship in it bought from Cyprus.

Joe had screamed over their backs, 'This is my house. Get out or I will call the police.'

The men left through the unsteady, folding gate, leaving greasy fingerprints on the dust-smoothened railing.

The maid left soon after. She took with her six wine glasses wrapped in newspaper, two ivory-carved photo frames and figurines of the Mother of God.

The whispers that came from the teakwood cupboard could still be heard, and Joe pressed his ears to the pillow. He shouted for three whole nights until the night watchman turned on the radio to its full volume. Crackle, scream, crackle, shout, song ... *tera jigar le liya, tuhje dil de diya* ... (I have taken your liver, I have given you my heart.)

Tap tap.

'*Aata hai,*' shouts Joe, and rushes to get the bread.

The *pavwala* was charitable to this man, whom he knew for years, with one free pav for breakfast and one free *pav* for dinner.

Joe cuts the pav into two, so it covers the space on the quarter plate, says his grace before meals, cleans his nose, and eats his meal. Dipping the pieces of bread gingerly in the ever-expanding boundary of gravy on the plate, he likes to attack its borders first.

Someone laughs downstairs.

'Ah! Don't laugh because she sent stew again. What do y'all eat at home eh, *dhoklas?*'

He shuts his ears with half of the *pav* still in his hand, curry around his fingers, when a large bunch of cackling people emerge from the building attached to the bungalow; a home till he lives, after which Joe's mother's would say it goes to Joe's nephew, who hardly visits, Joe's niece, who hardly cares, and Joe's brother's wife, who is dying.

'I will go see Martha,' Joe mumbles. 'I know the buses that go.'

❋

The next afternoon, the coconut gatherers are back. With *lungis* wrapped around their waists they clamber up the tree, hairy legs around tall barks. They begin hacking heavy bunches of coconuts and lower them down with a rope. The sweeper drags dried, hacked fronds through the dirt path, and stacks them in front of the rusted, sunk-to-the-earth gate for the garbage truck to come and take them away. This awakens Joe.

'How many times have I told you not to touch those coconuts?' he shouts.

The coconut gatherers turn to look at him and grin widely in the afternoon sun. They break open the top of a tender coconut and drink the soothing sweet water, letting drops trickle down their chin. They play throw-and-hop with the empty green shells, and punch each other playfully.

Joe has had enough.

He knots the drawstring of his knee-length pyjamas, and trundles down the corroding and its winding steps. He tiptoes through the dried leaves covering the dirt path until he reaches the heap of coconut. He looks around; his weak eye compensated by his strong eye, both compensated by a pair of thick black-framed glasses.

He finds a dried, brown coconut with its antlers lying at one end, grabs it and bangs it on the head of the coconut gatherer who was about to make his journey up the tree. Hard, again and again, as all the bones in his body unite to jut out from shrivelled white skin.

The other coconut gatherer grabs Joe from behind. He clutches his throat in his thick hands and pushes him down. Joe can feel a crack up his thin arm, as it makes a concave in wet mud. The injured coconut gatherer looks at him, offended, crouched under the tree, as he uses a rag to arrest the blood flowing from his oily, slick scalp.

Joe lies, limbs askew on the soil that his father had chosen many years ago to build a family home on. *Sweet Home,* they called it. Now the glazed name embedded in the front-wall of the house had faded and could hardly be read. Now the parapets crumble like stale cake, and expose the iron grids that hold them together.

Joe can smell the grass and the wet mud.

The first showers come down and drenched as he is, he — Joe Emmanuel Pereira — has taken action for the first time in his life.

Victor Rangel-Ribeiro, who was born in 1925 into a Goan family, had a grandmother who loved to tell him folk tales; everybody else loved to read. By the time he entered St. Xavier's College in Mumbai in 1941, he was writing his own stories and had read through most of the Victorian-era literature in the family bookcases. Among works by Somerset Maugham, Aldous Huxley, Graham Greene and George Bernard Shaw, he found books by three Indians, that changed his literary landscape forever — Mulk Raj Anand, R.K. Narayan, and Raja Rao. They evoked not just the sights and sounds but the very smell of Indian soil; he also discovered that the three authors wove the lives of individuals into that of a community so tightly that they were virtually inseparable. Mulk Raj, R.K. Narayan, and Raja Rao were all born in the first decade of the 20th century and lived on into the first decade of the 21st century; Victor's own writing career thus provides a link between the two eras, taking in also the careers of those who came in between, such as Bharati Mukherjee and Arundhati Roy. He is among the 136 authors listed in *South Asian Literature in English,* and the 53 in *South Asian Novelists in English.* Rangel-Ribeiro's debut novel *Tivolem* (Milkweed Editions, 1998) was named one of the twenty notable first novels to be published in America in 1998 and won him the Milkweed National Fiction Prize. The New York Foundation for the Arts awarded him its Fiction Fellowship in 1991. A member of MENSA since 1988, he is a trained musician, has covered classical music performances and opera for the New York Times, and was for three years music director of the Beethoven Society of New York. His books have found a place in the leading university libraries in the USA and also in Oxford and Cambridge. He now divides his time between Princeton and Goa, where he conducts writing and editing workshops, and also conducts the occasional concert.

Matters of the Heart

VICTOR RANGEL-RIBEIRO

Your letter today, Shakuntala, I did not need. I look forward daily to hearing from you, hurry to the table where the mail is kept when I see your tiny pale blue envelope waiting for me. A whiff of your perfume greets me each time I open one, and it did so again today; but you now write to say things are going sour? That we may not get married this year, after all? And because of what? Money? The number of bridesmaids? Where the wedding will be celebrated, and by whom? Yet, why am I angry with you? I know you better than that. Our times are still out of joint, if you and I have to be side-lined while our elders quibble over matters that do not matter at all. Tonight, I must write you a letter, a long, calm, unloverlike letter, analysing the situation we find ourselves in, and exploring our options.

If I were to write to you now, at this moment, instead of just sitting by my desk at the office thinking things out, what I inwardly feel and say would upset you no end. For I see nothing ahead of me — nothing. Behind me lie 23 years of loneliness and frustration, the years before I met you. And yet, my failure is surely not due to a lack of direction; for years now I have known exactly where I want to go, what I want to do. I want stability, and I want it soon. I want a home of my own. A wife. A wife and family. Plenty of children.

Do you realize what would happen if you were to write to me tomorrow, saying it's all over, finished? Can you see me tearing open that envelope with anxious fingers, and the look on my face as the news gets to me? How do you think I will react? Will I think back to lost opportunities, even to casual flings I might have had, if I had wanted to? What if you had written me such a letter a few weeks ago — would I then have gone off on the rebound, chasing after Grace? I am, after all, susceptible.

But enough of these thoughts; now I must focus on my work — that, at least, will be bring me some peace of mind, until my shift is over.

❋

Within the hour I get an unexpected call; I think it might be my editor, but it's from Grace, and she sounds depressed.

'Grace? You all right? How did the evening go?'

'Not well at all.'

'What!' I say, quite unfeelingly. 'Did you turn down the latest marriage proposal? What happened to the nights in Paris they promised you, the trip to the Silk Road, the moonlit camel ride to Samarkhand?'

'I spat on the camel driver,' she says.

'Oh,' I say, not knowing what else to say.

'Forget about that foolishness,' she says. "I want to move on. There's a poetry reading this evening. Seven o'clock. I'll be going. Care to come?'

'I'd love to, but ...'

'I thought you wanted to go to a reading.' She sounds more than a little disappointed. 'Now I hear a 'but.' What's going on in your mind?'

I have to think of what's going wrong with Shakuntala, that's what's going through my mind. And I'm thinking I should not be going out with you, much as I'd like to, because I'm in love with Shakuntala and yet I find you so attractive, I do not trust myself. How can I tell you that?

'It's going to be tight in the newsroom here tonight.' I tell her, which is absolutely true, but it's a bogus excuse, because I'm on the day shift, not on duty tonight.

'A tram will get you from your office to the reading in just five minutes. Can you spare an hour? Jibanananda Das will be reading his own poems.'

'The way you say the name, it sounds like a recommendation. Then why haven't I heard of him? Jibana who?'

'You haven't heard of him because he writes only in Bengali. But he is the most famous poet here after Tagore.'

'Then he'll be reading in Bengali, and I won't understand a thing. Sorry!'

'I'll translate for you, Stan,' she pleads. 'He's wonderful. Done, then? I'll meet you at your office.'

'I'll meet you at the reading instead. Where will that be?'

'45 Rahimtulla Road. Private home, quite large, white exterior, sits by itself to the right of the tram tracks, in the middle of what looks like a mini-park.'

'I'll be there.'

'Come before seven, as early as you can. I'll be there much before. I'll save a spot for you, but it will be crowded, you'll have to look for me.'

I'm taking the afternoon shift and put pressure on the subs to turn copy around faster. 'Speed and accuracy mark the professional,' I hector them. 'Move that pencil faster down those lines; push that pencil, your eyes will follow.' As soon as their edited copy hits my desk, I glance over it, hit the bell for the peon, send it down to the press to be set in type. My desk has never been cleaner.

Ananda, who has come in early as usual to take over the night shift, notices. 'Is this the new you, or are you planning to duck out of here early today?'

'Both.'

'So what's up?'

'I'm going to a poetry reading. Jibosomething Das, said to be famous.'

'Jibananda! Yes, he is famous. But he writes and he'll read in Bengali, so you won't understand a thing. Too bad I can't go with you and translate.'

'I've got me a translator.'

'If he's good, you'll have a memorable evening.'

'Now I'm sure it will be.' I don't have to tell him it's Grace.

'Then I take it, it's a woman! You old hound dog! Why don't you go now?' Ananda says. 'I can take over right away.'

Wonderful! That will give me time to be with Grace before the reading begins. We can have a pleasant time together, perhaps even make plans to go to other readings. But then that thought itself gives me pause — I need to back off, before I mess up other lives and mine. Standing Grace up will be a kindness, absolutely the right thing to do.

'Thanks for the offer, Ananda, but I've changed my mind; I'm staying. There'll be other readings, and I'll pick one when you and I can go together.'

'Rubbish,' he says. 'I didn't mean to discourage you. Go, soak in the atmosphere. We Bengalis do things very differently here than in the rest of India. When you hear Jibananda read, you may not understand a word he says, but watch those near you, how he holds them spellbound. Make mental notes. Years from now, when you write a novel about your stay in Gangapur, you'll be able to put that scene in.'

The murmur of voices and muted sounds of tabla and sitar greet me as I walk up a winding path that leads to the reading site. The front door is open; the walls of the vestibule are lined with shoe racks that rise to almost seven feet above floor level. I have to stand on tiptoe to put my shoes away. The music is filtering through a door to my right; I pry it slowly open to find a dimly lit room packed almost to capacity with people sitting cross-legged on the floor. A few dozen latecomers stand packed in a crowd along the back wall. Sure, Grace had said she would save a spot for me, but where is she in this crowd? And then, four rows up and close to the side, I see her waving.

Miraculously, people make room for me to get through; I have to move gingerly between bodies and limbs, whispering apologies every step of the way. Sitting down is an occasion for more embarrassment; Grace giggles even as she helps me maintain my balance on the way down. Finally I'm wedged beside her, our bodies touching.

'Jibanananda will be reading as soon as the music ends,' she whispers encouragingly, but the music shows no signs of ending; the woman sitar player is deep in an endless stream of variations, and the tabla player, head nodding in time to his rhythms, is egging her on.

'*Khup!*' cry people in the audience, showing their approval. Others keep on chatting, mindlessly. Grace turns to me and smiles; she gives my hand a squeeze. I squeeze back, smile.

I know just enough about Indian classical music to figure out that when the sitarist and the tabla player both go into a frenzy, they are nearing the end — or it is no more than fifteen minutes or so away. And so it ends, with garlands for both musicians, and much bowing with folded hands; and then two men walk on to the platform, to loud applause; both are wearing shawls around their neck, but I know at once which one is the poet. He has to be the diffident one.

'That's Jibanananda,' Grace says, confirming my hunch as she points him out to me, her eyes shining. 'Oh, isn't he the dreamer!'

The emcee picks up a microphone, tests the acoustics, asks for the volume to be increased. Satisfied at last that his voice is now bouncing off the walls, he rambles on, with much gesticulation, pointing every so often to the poet now seated beside him. Grace listens intently, but is soon bored.

'The usual piffle,' she whispers. 'Extravagant praise. I'll tell you later.' The dreadfully loud monotone, the heat, the closeness of the atmosphere would have gotten to me, but there's a warm body right next to mine, and each time it moves, however slightly, unsettling thoughts go swirling through my head. To distract myself I imagine what might be going on in Jibanananda's head. Apparently, nothing; his gaze occasionally flicks over the audience, but his face is immobile. It is plain to me that he is paying absolutely no attention to what is being said about him. Occasionally, when applause breaks out, he acknowledges it, and smiles. At such times Grace and I, too, turn our faces towards each other and smile, amusedly. Our faces are so close, our lips could graze in passing. Has she caught my thought? She looks at me wide-eyed, and I quickly turn away.

Prolonged applause tells me the speechifying is over. I turn to see the old man has bent over and clasped the poet by the shoulders, and is gently helping him to rise.

Jibanananda does not immediately begin to recite his poetry; instead, he greets old friends in the audience, introduces close relatives, answers some banter and stray questions tossed from the floor. All this Grace translates for me. And then Jibanananda himself asks a question. 'He wants to know what we would like to hear first,' Grace says.

There's a roar from the crowd.

'They're asking for *'Banalata'*,' Grace says.

'And what's that?'

'His most famous poem, about a mysterious woman called Banalata Sen.'

'A love poem?'

'Not exactly. Nobody knows, but it could be.'

The poet gestures for silence, but when he speaks again it creates another commotion.

'He says they have heard it often enough, and they can hear it at the end,' Grace interprets. 'And his fans are telling him, he can read it now, and read it again at the end. Now let's listen.'

The house falls silent.

'Move your head closer,' she says softly, 'so I can whisper in your ear, without upsetting others.'

Jibananda's voice is soft and mellifluous, there's poetry in just the sound of it, even though I cannot understand a word. Grace translates the rolling phrases in snippets. Her warm breath now fanning my cheek, now pulsing in my ear, distracts me from much of what she is saying, but some of the lines come through:

She brought me peace, Banalata Sen from Natore.

The why and how not important; Banalata Sen, bringing peace, like a dove.

Her hair dark like a night in Vidisa;
Sravasti had sculpted her face …
I looked at her in the darkness.
She said: 'Where have you been all my life?'

That is Banalata's question, but why do I feel Grace is addressing it to me? Is it because her hair is brushing against my cheek, her eyes are locked onto mine, because our breaths are mingled and our lips so close together once again that now we could kiss almost without moving? One little move would give me heaven and hell all at once. I must get out of here, out into the fresh air and the coolness of the night, while I still have the will.

All around us the people are clapping wildly, the poem has ended; some are crying. Are those tears I see in Grace's eyes as well?

'Must get back to work,' I whisper. 'Didn't expect the music, took too long. Talk to you tomorrow.'

We hold hands a moment, then she lets go. The man to my left turns his body slightly to let me pass. In my haste to leave I'm less careful how I move as I stumble towards the exit. Each person I tread on I touch with my fingertips, in a mute gesture of apology. Nobody gets angry. At the door I pause a moment to look at her; I

sense that she knows that I'm looking at her, but she will not turn
her head. And then I'm out in the vestibule, reclaiming my shoes,
and though I'm a very long way from where I'm staying I decide to
walk all the way rather than take the tram. Perhaps the cool air will
calm my thoughts.

Hair like a dark night in Vidisa.

This is a strange part of town for me and at the first intersection
I pause to get my bearings. A street to the right seems promising,
and I take it; though not as broad as the avenue I'm on, it curves to
the north-east, and might save me quite a few steps.

Sravasti had sculpted her face.

Who sculpted yours, Grace?

A few hundred yards further down, a broken street lamp, and
then another, make me question the wisdom of my choice. The
neighbourhood is getting seedier. If I'm going to turn back, it has
to be now, before things get much worse. But straight ahead and
not too far away I see the bright glow of a major intersection. Dare
I chance it?

Vidisa. Her hair. Her face.

I remind myself that I've been in worse situations in Dharghat;
the last time a dusk-to-dawn curfew had been imposed there, during
the riots of '47, I had had to walk home for miles through darkened
neighbourhoods that changed from Hindu to Muslim and back to
Hindu again. A policeman who checked my pass had given me some
sound advice: 'Walk in the middle of the street,' he said. 'Stick to the
main roads. You are wearing white, that makes you more visible in
the pitch darkness, makes the mawalis think you're a friend, since
you're not afraid. If you show any fear, you're a dead man.'

From here to those lights can be no more than six hundred
steps or so. I'll walk briskly down the middle of the street, staying
alert, I mean to stay alive.

Where have you been all my life?

The night is full of awakenings and finally at five I throw on some clothes and step out into the dank morning air. The roads have just been washed clean, and there are small puddles of water everywhere. Where should I go? The sidewalks glisten with reflected luminescence. I decide to follow my feet, which in turn decide to follow my nose. This way and that I go, following the hint of baking bread here, the aroma of fresh ground coffee there. But it is neither bakery nor coffee shop that finally draws me in. Instead, directly in front of me, stretches the lighted interior of a church, candles flickering on the main altar. The church itself is empty, save for a couple of shadowy figures praying in the nave.

Almost mechanically, I, who have not been inside a place of worship since Christmas, walk in the door and genuflect before taking a seat. And there I sit, while memories of past masses and litanies, past sermons, past weddings, Magnificats, funerals and 'Te Deum' flood unbidden into my mind. I remember little of what was preached from the pulpit. In those days the priests spoke mostly of fire and brimstone, but their voices were too loud, and their message too unforgiving, for me to believe they truly spoke for God. But the settings have remained fixed in reality as they have remained fixed in my mind — always there are the tall candles, and always, if one waits long enough, there come the whiffs of incense, spiralling thinly into the air. Ah yes, I do remember one funeral oration, for an uncle of mine, because the words that were being spoken bore little relation to the man I knew in life. Even better I remember an unspoken tribute to my father, who died when I was ten, and an old violinist friend played over his casket the Meditation from Thais. Normally he played with a scratchy tone and faltering fingers, but that day it seemed to me that he played with the soul of an angel; it made me cry.

There must be angels around me now, in this house of God, and more saints than are visible in the niches in the walls. The priest is saying Mass, and God must be here, invisible as always, though we ourselves are too visible to God. Visible and transparent, we and our past, and our future as well. But if I were to ask God, between Grace and Shakuntala, whom should I choose, would God answer me, or tell me to exercise my free will? Probably the latter. So following that advice, let me think of Shakuntala first, because I knew her first. But does it really matter whom I knew first, when both are now present in my life? What I'm thinking about now, is my life, not just the two people I'm in love with, supposing for the moment that what I'm feeling for Grace is truly love. What I feel for Shakuntala is love; of that I'm absolutely sure. I feel protective of her. If that isn't love, what is? Am I in love with Grace? I said I was, didn't I, a moment ago? But it could be just infatuation. I'm dazzled by her, by her sharp intellect, her quick wit. Is this then a choice between beauty on the one hand, and brains on the other? What if the beauty fades? What if the brains curdle, the wit turns sour? If the good qualities fade, what will be left?

It is at the moment that I pose this question that God begins to speak to me. 'You forget that it is not just a matter of your free will,' God says, 'but theirs as well. These two women that you speak about, they have a choice to make as well. Sooner or later the matter will be resolved, either by you making a choice, or one or both of them making it for you. Which of you three should take the initiative? I cannot guide you in this, God tells me, because if I did, you would feel obliged to follow my directive; even though I had not stripped you of your free will, you would think I had. You are concerned right now about making the right choice, God said to me, so you may wind up making no choice at all. But should you make one, you will not know whether you made the right one until it is too late. At the very end of your life you may wonder, what if I had picked the other one? What if? And you will be tempted to imagine having made the other choice, and you will paint that picture in richer colours than you paint the life you have actually been living; but that picture will be false, because you will not really know how that would have turned out. It's your choice, God said, I want no part of it.

Thanks for nothing, God, I say. Does that sound ungracious to you?

The priest turns and gives me his blessing.

'Go,' he says. 'the Mass has ended.'

Augusto do Rosário Rodrigues the author (1910–1999), was a regular contributor of poems and short stories in Portuguese to the post-1961 Goan press and radio. A collection of his stories, entitled *Contos Regionais* (Regional Tales), was published in 1987. Characterised by the Goan critic Bailon de Sá as displaying a sort of 'inside out exoticism,' his fiction, often historical, focuses on the Goan Catholic community and treats themes of decline, re-evaluation and recovery.

Paul Melo e Castro the translator, is an academic and lecturer in Comparative Literature and Portuguese at the University of Glasgow. He has research interests in literature, film and visual culture, and is currently engaged in research projects on the post-1961 Goan short story and on postcolonial photography. He has a substantial body of scholarly writing particularly in the area of translation. His publications include *Lengthening Shadows: An Anthology of Goan Short Stories translated from the Portuguese* Volume I and II (Goa 1556, 2016). He is also the author of *Shades of Grey: 1960s Lisbon in Novel, Film and Photography.* (London: MHRA Texts and Dissertations, 2011). He lives in Edinburgh, with his partner and children.

You Can Never Be Too Careful

Translated from the Portuguese to English

AUGUSTO DO ROSÁRIO RODRIGUES

TRANSLATED BY PAUL MELO E CASTRO

Sancho Serapião do Santo Sepulcro Costa Paredes Malcorado, son of old Nicomedes, the sacristan of Santa Eufrásia, had just entered his twentieth year. He had rudimentary schooling, a basic knowledge of music, and knew how to assist at Mass. His family had inherited land from a great-great-grandfather missionary, which they lived well off, though without ostentation. Nicomedes, besides village sacristan, was also headman, justice of the peace, and chief castrator of the local pigs, and wanted his boy to follow in his four-fold footsteps.

Sancho, however, had far loftier ambitions: he planned to strike it rich in Africa, so he could come back and vie with the grandees of the village. When his parents passed on, leaving their house in the hands of a maiden aunt, our hero availed himself of an offer from a neighbour with a tailor's shop in Beira and went over to work for him as an accountant. As well as bed and board he earned three hundred escudos per month. The tailor, a widower with a single daughter of marriageable age, treated him like a son. God willing — the tailor thought — Sancho will join the family one day. His daughter, dusky-skinned and lovely, had finished high school and acquired an almost aristocratic bearing. Yet our haughty son of a sacristan, vain of his status as a village *gaunkar,* looked upon his host with nothing but disdain. The tailor, realising his daughter deserved better than a sacristan for a father-in-law, soon got shot of the uppity blighter.

Our hero, who had some money put aside, continued on to Lourenço Marques where he found a job as a customs broker for an English firm, earning two thousand escudos a month. On the QT he traded in cloth, which quickly augmented his nest egg. But what really ensured his prosperity was the reclusive life he led. Due to his caste snobbery, the local Goans, few of whom were of his kind, fled this unsociable boor. And so he lived alone, cooking for himself, untroubled by bothersome visitors. His frugal ways trebled his capital and his culinary skills encased his stout body in an ample layer of flab.

One fine day, after totting up his accounts, he found that he now had nine thousand escudos safely stashed in the Banco Nacional Ultramarino. He smiled with delight, ate six *chouriços* and four eggs for lunch, topped that off with a generous nip of firewater, and took himself to bed. When he awoke, he decided to transfer his savings with the Ultramarino to its branch in Goa. The next morning, this issue with the bank resolved, he packed his bags, dispatched a telegram to his aunt, and left on a steamer for Bombay.

On that torrid March morning, the inhabitants of Santa Eufrásia found themselves at a loss. A hulking great gorilla, freshly shaven, a pair of sunglasses perched on his bulbous nose, a pith helmet atop his head, had climbed down from a gharry with several cases, a caged parrot, and a wolfhound. As he had alighted at the door of Nicomedes, the rubberneckers sidled up for a closer peek. It turned out to be an almost spherical man sucking on a cigar. Squeezed into a woollen suit, he flaunted both a hideous Ngungunyane-like belly and a gold-handled walking sick. It was, of course, Sancho, whom no one recognised. Even his terror-stricken aunt hightailed it as he and the driver brought the luggage up onto the *balcão* … Over the coming days, the *africanista*, primped in flame-red pyjamas, sat and waited in vain for the four grandees of the village — the priest, the doctor, the teacher and the headman — to call. He even had the house whitewashed and decked the walls with garish prints. The old chairs were repaired and varnished, while the old sideboard dating from the time of his great-great-grandfather, the missionary, flaunted ostrich eggs and a collection of bizarre seashells.

The only people to come were the grocer and the tavern keeper, who were lavishly treated to gin and those awful cigars. And so tales of the wealth of Nicomedes's son reached the villages. The grocer and tavern keeper, whom Sancho's aunt had offered a little sweetener to find a match for her nephew, spread the word far and wide. Now the baker and the fishwife gossiped about the thousands of rupees that Sancho had brought back, described his house, his furniture, his gold-handled walking stick. But this boosterism had no effect: everyone who clapped eyes on Sancho thought himself gripped by a macabre daydream.

A notice in the papers announcing the return to his mansion in Santa Eufrásia of his excellency *senhor* Sancho Malcorado, senior manager with an English firm based in Lourenço Marques, also raised no interest whatsoever. Sancho's poor aunt was greatly put out, having expected a flood of proposals for her nephew, but no one gave a hoot. The grocer, who had spent some time in Panjim rooming with a tailor cousin, was of the opinion that Sancho should frequent the Clube, where he could have his pick of winsome damsels who would knock the doctor's daughter, and her fifty-thousand-rupee dowry, into a cocked hat.

'Speaking frankly,' said the *africanista*, 'I don't need a dowry; what I want is a woman with endowments. I've got loads of money. I could buy this whole village with a snap of my fingers.'

A few days later, the tavern keeper came by with a goldsmith, a skilful marriage broker much sought-after all over Goa. While the drawn-out proceedings got underway, our moneyed protagonist joined the capital's most eclectic club, which was getting ready for a gala ball.

Togged up in a hideous smoking jacket that reached down to his knees, a dark pince-nez clamped to his globular nose, perfumed and slathered in Brilliantine, our wealthy hero strode haughtily into the ballroom. When the youngsters saw this uber-scarecrow, who ogled the ladies' bare shoulders like a bumpkin, they all sniggered dismissively. Sancho shot back with an obscene gesture, which escaped no one's notice. His mooncalf smile, revealing two gold canines in a cavernous maw, proved unable to erase the affront and the boys immediately christened him Sancho Panza Malcriado. But Sancho took the situation in his stride. Spotting a limp-looking woman of forty or so gazing out at the dance floor, he ambled over and tried to make a 180-degree bow. His abdominous promontory saw matters differently, however, and the son of Nicomedes had to content himself with a brief nod.

That dance was martyrdom for the unfortunate lady. Sancho clasped her waist with his left hand and clung on till the number was over, boasting that he'd been the best dancer at the Clube Girassol in Lourenço Marques. This marvellous twinkle-toes, stomping away as if to the beat of an African drum, kicked almost every other couple on the dance floor, barking many a shin and ripping not a few dresses.

Feeling himself subject to the censure and scorn of those present, Santa Eulália's Sancho Panza slunk off and posted himself where he could ambush the trays of food and drink passing back and forth across the room. He tried the lot like a little boy. A while later, waistline dilated and spirits raised, he slouched on a sofa tucked back into one corner and let his stomach do its work. At length, a gentleman of a certain age approached and asked for a light before asking, with great discretion, whether Sancho was new to the Clube.

Sancho peered down from the towering height of his rupees and retorted in a peevish voice: 'And who might you be, illustrious gentleman I've never met? A policeman?' And he gave a moronic cackle that showed him up for what he was: a barely literate countryman, a thoughtless oaf.

'I do apologise. Mr … ? Mr … ?'

'Sancho Malcorado, senior manager with an English firm based in Lourenço Marques.'

'Nepomuceno Furtado at your service, a humble medical officer, now retired.'

'Well, doctor, the party was a blast but the catering left a lot to be desired. Over in Lourenço Marques, if there's no *bacalhau* or *vinho verde* at a do they think it's a damp squib.'

'Wife not with you?'

'Not married, pal. Been looking for wife in vain for six months, pal. And my, aren't the popsies here flighty bints. Over in Africa everyone has a *mulata* on the side.'

Dr Furtado gave a thin smile. So this was the groom that much-vaunted goldsmith was trying to fob off on his daughter! You can never be too careful with touted husbands.

SHORT MEMOIRS

Ahmed Bunglowala is the creator of Shorty Gomes, India's iconic private eye of Goan origin. His publications include *The Days and Nights of Shorty Gomes* (Rupa, 1993) and *Shorty Gomes: Vintage Indian Crime Stories* (Goa 1556, 2015). Ahmed was born in Bombay (now Mumbai) where he spent his formative years. He now lives in Goa doing as little as possible. He writes crime fiction, memoir and short stories. He is an enthusiastic cook and an advocate of healthy eating.

Bombay Blues

AHMED BUNGLOWALA

From 1975 to 1983, we lived on Pedder Road, Bombay, as paying guests. Vijaya and I were recently married and the one-room-bath-kitchenette accommodation suited us fine — especially after the few months we had spent in a shabby and claustrophobic place in Kurla East, with a nosey landlord as bonus. What hastened our exit from the Kurla place was that one day a chunk of the ceiling plaster came crashing down. Fortunately, no one was hurt.

The landlady at Pedder Road was a jaded and quirky film star of yesteryears and my first meeting with her had evoked a strong association with Gloria Swanson's character in Billy Wilder's *Sunset Boulevard*. She (the landlady) had advertised the PG room in the TOI. We had become voracious readers of the 'accommodation available' columns after the plaster falling incident. I had written her a postcard saying I was interested and would like to check out the place. She had phoned me after a couple of weeks and I went over to meet her. She looked at me with her cat-like green eyes, sizing me up. The usual interrogation followed. Soon, she agreed quite readily to rent the place to us. I was thrilled, and paid out a month's rent in advance. Before leaving she let me know that the one thing that had greatly weighed in my favour was my handwriting — it was neat and clean, she said. Later, I was to understand that a good hand is the written equivalent of a good voice.

Soon we settled down in our new digs — we bought a second-hand fridge, an old cassette player and a pre-owned Jawa motorcycle; not all of them at the same time. So we were feeling pretty good about our lives — we had cold beer and ham in the fridge, Leonard Cohen, Bob Dylan and Joan Baez for company, and our 250 cc bike for easy mobility to film screenings, beaches and friends' houses — from Colaba to Versova.

One of the things our hidebound landlady was very particular about was the doorbell ringing 'protocol'.

Our visitors, she insisted, had to ring the doorbell twice. Hers, once. Easier said than done. And this became a constant source of irritation and friction. On weekends, our small place would invariably turn into an adda with many of our friends simply forgetting the golden rule. Holy cow! The arguments over recently watched movies at the Alliance Francaise or Max Müller would grow progressively more boisterous. Vijaya and I would try, in vain, to coax our friends to keep the decibel levels low. The impromptu bar in the kitchen would be depleted by midnight and every one would make their way home after grabbing a few bites of the food that someone had brought along — very often kebabs and *naans* from Sarvi in Nagpada. Bombay, at that time, was flush with creative energy — in cinema, theatre, poetry and fiction. It was a very stimulating period in our lives.

Our eclectic mix of friends included writers, poets, journalists, academics, film buffs and even a private detective, for good measure. Her name was Keya Dutt, who was to become one of our dearest friends during that time. We would often go to her place in Andheri on my Jawa to while away the hours in the company of her friends — all Bengalis — and listening to Keya's exploits about her matrimonial snooping on husbands cheating on their wives, and wives cheating on their husbands. At that time, cheating on your spouse seemed like a fairly alien concept to Vijaya and me! That would change as time went by. The culprit was I. I was working for a 'diversified' Sindhi-owned company that among other things, exported beef to the Middle East and imported pacemakers into India. At work, I got involved briefly with a female colleague and all hell broke loose. Vijaya walked out on me and stayed with her parents in Chembur for a couple of weeks. Some of our good mutual friends got into action and helped in dousing the flames and saving our marriage. Thank God, for that. Never again, I wowed.

Back to happier times in our little room in Pedder Road. It was crammed with big black-and-white posters of Groucho Marx, Humphrey Bogart and Marilyn Monroe taped on the walls. These collectors' items, brought from Paris by another dear friend, Edwina Alva, got sadly misplaced in the many relocations that were to follow in our lives. We met Edwina at St. Xavier's College, Bombay, where we studied, at an enchanted time in the history of this iconic institution. We had even got married in Edwina's apartment in Colaba, while her father was at work. A deputy from the Marriage Registrar's Office presided over the simple ceremony, with a room-full of supportive friends and *one* solo close relative, my to-be brother-in-law. Our 'civil' marriage formalities were over in half an hour, which was followed by catered biryani and some unremarkable wine. Edwina would, later on, very graciously agree to become the godmother of our two children. Bravo!

In February 1983, our son Akil was born. Soon, the PG room was too small for an active, fast-crawling baby. That's when we decided to move to Pune, with a job with an eccentric Parsi company where everyone was *strictly* addressed by their first names. We were coming to grips with life in the slow lane in Pune, a city dubbed a 'pensioners' paradise' and the Oxford of the East. We were neither students, nor retired people, and for the first few months we sorely missed our many friends in Bombay and our small, lively, smoke-filled room on Pedder Road, where our friends were expected, like the postman, to ring twice to avoid a chilling confrontation with our landlady with the cat-like green eyes.

Vijaya and I made some new friends in Pune and gradually got used to life in the slow lane. Our children — our son, a rolling stone, and our daughter, a would-be dancer, went through school and college and now they were on the threshold of deciding what to do with their lives as young adults. We hoped, like all parents, they would do well for themselves and not lose their moral bearings.

Fast forward to 2010. We were busy packing our precious books and DVDs for our move to Goa after my retirement from the Parsi company. Ironically, we had decided to leave Pune, the 'pensioners' paradise', which an architect friend described as, 'a sprawl without a centre or a soul.' Goa, we thought, like so many others, would centre and provide us with new direction and dimension.

In the 1970s and '80s there was an overnight ship service between Bombay and Goa and back. We had taken a round trip on this ship once with baby Akil in our arms. Travel on this 'slow' ship was a magical experience. People would be drinking, singing, chatting or simply gazing at the stars. Goa, in those days, was as close as you could get to the idea of paradise. Today there is a sea change. Rapacious mining (now suspended), mass tourism and reckless 'development' have taken a heavy toll. Corruption, greed and drugs are rampant (cocaine, anyone?). The small, verdant state is literally choking on garbage strewn all over the place. It also has a seamy reputation for sex tourism; paedophilia is practically on the menus of some of the beach shacks. The writing on the wall is clear for anyone to see — a soiled and bruised paradise, if you ever saw one. But the complicit politicians and other powerful lobbies are in brazen denial. As Shorty Gomes, the sardonic, rum-drinking private eye ruefully observes: *Crime now sits in high places — insular and mocking.* It still does. Even higher. Well, that's another story.

How are Vijaya and I faring in Goa? Not bad. We have made some new friends, have cultivated a taste for feni and fish-curry-rice, and have learnt to appreciate the charms of the Goa monsoon. Doesn't sound like much? Maybe, you're right. We now live in a big Goan house in a village in Bardez, but still sometimes feel nostalgic about our start-up days in the small room on Pedder Road, where life was a heady mix of ideas and self-exploration. The persistence of memory? Must learn to let go of it. Or should I?

Yvonne Vaz Ezdani spent her childhood in Burma, the beautiful land of pagodas. She still cherishes the memories: school days, falling in love, marriage and motherhood. Some unpleasant memories too form part of this period of her life. She lost her left arm in a dacoity incident. Her spirit embraced it all. She left Burma for Goa, India, in 1982. Some years later, she became a widow much too young. Through these difficult times, she matured. Looking back, she feels a sense of achievement in the many roles she has assumed as a teacher, later a counsellor to teenagers, and most importantly as a mother to two beautiful daughters. She is the author of two books, *Songs of the Survivors* (Goa 1556, 2007), and *New Songs of the Survivors* (Speaking Tiger, 2015) with a foreword by Amitav Ghosh which shed light on the Goan diaspora in Burma. She now spends her time between Brisbane, Australia, with her family, and Goa, feeling blest and doing the things that make her happy.

The Bayingyi People of Burma

Yvonne Vaz Ezdani

It was 1970 and I was a young student at Rangoon University in Burma (now Myanmar). Among my many friends and hostel-mates, Cecelia D'Silva intrigued me the most. Tall, slim and grey-eyed, she was noticeably different from the others in appearance, although there was nothing foreign in her Burmese accent or in her behaviour. She told me she came from the Bayingyi community, descendants of the Portuguese, many of whom had come from Goa a few hundred years ago, and had settled in the valley of the Mu River where she lived. She also described the place as a colony of Catholics.

My curiosity was aroused.

We Goans had Portuguese connections too. I had visited Goa as a child with my family in the 1950s and I knew that it was ruled by the Portuguese. My Goan grandfather held a Portuguese passport before he took Indian citizenship. We knew a Goan family named D'Silva in Burma and they looked more brown, more Indian than European. I realised that the common factor between Goans and Bayingyis was the Portuguese, but I still couldn't connect the dots.

I wanted to find out more about the Bayingyi people.

Myanmar writer and historian, Than Myint-U, writes that in Burma, the 'Europeans were initially labelled "Bayingyis", a Burmese corruption of the Arabic *farenji*.[1] The word was applied mainly to the Portuguese, the European people with whom the

---

1. Farenji is derived of the Arabic or Persian word for Franks (Western Europeans).

Burmese had the most contact.' Much later on, the word Bayingyi also took on the connotation of Roman Catholic, but now it refers mainly to the Luso-descendants.

There was no internet in those days and most of the standard history books in the library were written from a mainstream Burmese perspective. There was some content on the Portuguese in Burma in the sixteenth and seventeenth centuries; however, most of the Burmese history of that period was about palace conspiracies and battles between kings of various states and kingdoms of Burma. There were brief references to the Portuguese pirates who roamed the coastal cities of Burma and sired 'half-breeds' who were absorbed into the local population. But these descriptions did not seem to apply to the Portuguese settlers in the district of Central Burma that my friend had told me about. However, there was one recurring Portuguese name in the books with regard to this early period: Filipe de Brito, whose Burmese nickname was Nga Zinga. What caught my attention was a reference to the Portuguese man's strong and beautiful wife — Luísa de Brito — who played an important role in Bayingyi history. One of the books I consulted said she had been born in Goa. Again, Goa was mentioned as the place from which the Portuguese supply ships set sail to Burma. Ah-ha, I thought to myself — I had established the connection between Portugal, Goa, and Burma.

Strong women leaders fascinate me, and my desire to know more about Luísa de Brito has remained with me all these years. Recently, I have learnt more about her from the internet and from published books.

How did she become a leader of her people? It began with young Filipe de Brito e Nicote, who came to Arakan/Rakhine, via Goa, as a cabin boy in search of fame and fortune in the 1550s. He was a shrewd charmer who did business on the side and acquired substantial wealth. His flamboyant personality caught the attention of the Rakhine king, Minyazagyi, who appointed him as a palace guard. On one occasion de Brito protected the king from being killed in a palace conspiracy, and as a reward he was made Governor of Syriam. At the time Syriam, a port town, was the trade centre of Burma. Over time, de Brito became wealthy and powerful. His skilled Portuguese gunners fought battles for the Rakhine king and his network of spies helped acquire valuable information. Burma, then, was fragmented into several different kingdoms, each striving to gain more land and wealth, and Portuguese mercenaries became increasingly involved in the power struggles of the Burmese kings.

De Brito was arrogant and did not heed directives from Goa, the seat of Portuguese power in Asia. Yet, the *Estado da Índia* and the Church supported his self-proclaimed glory, probably because they thought he would contribute to Portuguese supremacy and conversions to Christianity in Burma. Power went to his head, and around 1602 he proclaimed himself King of Syriam. In Burma, the Portuguese mercenaries became unreliable and troublesome, causing the Rakhine king to regard them as foes rather than friends. De Brito made another enemy as well. The king of Ava, Anaukphetlun, wanted Natshinnaung, the king of Toungoo killed, but de Brito protected him in his fort at Syriam. Anaukphetlun and his army laid siege to Syriam and demanded the surrender of Natshinnaung. De Brito's loyalty to Natshinnaung who had converted to Christianity (rumour had it that he had secretly married de Brito's cousin) was so great that, at the cost of his own safety, he fought the Ava army and its allies. After a long drawn out siege, on March 29, 1613, de Brito conceded defeat. He was impaled on a sharp bamboo pole and, with his entrails hanging out, he was kept upright on the pole for all to see. He remained alive, in agony, for three days.

At the time, many Burmese Buddhists believed that Filipe de Brito brought a curse upon himself because he desecrated the Shwedagon Pagoda by dismantling the Dhammazedi Bell. The bell was believed to be the largest ever cast in bronze, measuring about 12 cubits high by eight cubits wide. It was kept in the Shwedagon, the most sacred Buddhist pagoda in Burma. In 1608, de Brito removed the bell from the sacred site and attempted to take it on a raft from Dagon (as Rangoon was known at that time) to Syriam. His plan was to melt the bell down and use the bronze to build cannons. This was not to be. The weight of the bell caused the raft to break, sinking both. Many attempts have been made to retrieve the Dhammazedi Bell, but without success. It is believed to be under 25 feet of mud.

The other legend associated with de Brito's death is that he breathed his last only after his wife, the exquisitely dark-haired, golden complexioned Dona Luísa de Brito *née* de Saldanha arrived by ship from Goa and embraced his feet amidst the wounded and dead Portuguese littered on the ground. Luísa was a broken woman in her grief. Yet, her strong personality resurfaced when she refused the Rakhine king's advances to make her his queen; she endured the torture that followed with dignity. There were more than 2,000 Portuguese captives — men, women, and children in the camp — and they all looked up to Luísa as their leader. Among the prisoners there were two priests, Father Diogo Nunes and Father Manoel de Fonseca, who kept the inmates' Catholic faith alive. Luísa's request to bury her husband was granted, and she was provided the resources for building a monument over his grave. This monument still stands today in Syriam, now known as Thanlyin in Burmese.

The victorious king decided to move the Portuguese prisoners from Syriam to his capital in Ava. They were made to march 500 miles and also made dangerous crossings over the Pegu River on rafts. Many died on the way and were buried on land with makeshift wooden crosses to mark their graves. It must have been sad for Luísa and the others to bury their departed family members so far from home in graves that would be erased in a short time. They knew that they too would never see home again. In his book, *Cannon Soldiers of Burma* (2014), James Myint Swe writes of the perilous journey between Syriam and Ava, following the historical account given by Father de Fonseca.

After their resettlement in Ava, many Portuguese men married local women, and established homes of their own. Weddings were celebrated by the two priests in their group, and the intermarriages were also solemnized in Buddhist monasteries. Others stayed in the camp where they survived on the little food that was provided to them. The young, able-bodied men were made to serve in the Burmese army.

Later, the new king of Ava, Thalun, decided to free the Portuguese and gave them land. Possibly, this happened because of the outspoken courage and determined efforts of Luísa. From Ava to Sagaing, then across from the east of the Mu River to its west bank, they travelled again, filled with joy that they were prisoners no more, although there were restrictions against their departure from the country. Over the course of time, their relations with the Burmese turned friendly, making them feel more secure. Their population had now increased to nearly 2,400, and they had a place to call home. They first built a small church, and then the elders marked out plots for individual houses. Luísa named their settlement Rio Aldeia — village by the river. Some families established villages at other points along the Mu River, which led into the Two Rivers Valley. There were more intermarriages with Burmese from neighbouring villages, and in a few years, the Portuguese settlers became culturally Burmese though they remained loyal to their Catholic faith and traditions. King Thalun sent them money to build churches and invited priests from Portugal, France, and Italy to conduct religious services there.

The Portuguese/Bayingyi soldiers who served in the Burmese army were now considered loyal subjects. They were no longer mercenaries or mere captives. For four hundred years, their descendants continued to serve as valued cannon-operators and gunners who defended the Burmese kingdom patriotically. Centuries later, when the British invaded Mandalay Palace in 1885, the Bayingyi soldiers defended the ruling King Thibaw until he ordered them to surrender.

Luísa de Brito, the matriarch, lived well into her seventies and was mourned by all the Bayingyi villagers when she died. Her indomitable spirit was remembered by the Bayingyi people for many centuries. Probably because of his wife's legacy, Filipe de Brito is still regarded as a hero among the Bayingyi people. Hero or renegade, de Brito lives on in Burmese history books and Bayingyi oral history.

The Luso-descendants of Burma have defied the loss of their identity and continue to live in the area along the Mu River, their main occupation being fishing and rice cultivation. Through oral transfer of knowledge, from one generation to the next, they are aware of their origins and, although they have adopted Burmese surnames along with their Christian given names, they still practice their Christian faith in a predominantly Buddhist society. Many of the Bayingyis are proud of the fact that they bear European features. Today, there are a number of Catholic priests and bishops from the Bayingyi community. Old baptism records and names on gravestones in the region bear Portuguese surnames. Though no one there speaks the Portuguese language any more, some Portuguese hymns are still sung at church services. As in the old days, a spirit of solidarity prevails among the Bayingyi villagers — everyone is the other's cousin, uncle, or aunt. Harvesting and threshing of paddy is still done as a community and the produce from the fields is shared among them. Sausages and a few sweet dishes that the Bayingyis make are similar to those made in Portugal and Goa.

I have no idea where my friend Cecilia is today. I only know she married her Goan boyfriend, a D'Souza, and later went abroad. I would not be surprised if they reside in Portugal now.[2]

---

2. Sources for this article:
    i.   James Myint Swe, *Cannon Soldiers of Burma*, Canada, 2014. Swe is a Bayingyi who migrated to Canada. Certain facts presented have been verified by Yvonne Ezdani through correspondence with James Myint Swe.
    ii. Thant Myint-U, *The Making of Modern Burma*, Cambridge University Press, 2001.
    iii. Luis Nestor and Joaquim de Castro, *Bayingy: The Hidden Face of Burma*, Youtube, 2012; a documentary on the Bayingyi sponsored by the Macau International Institute.

Reena Martins has been a journalist with leading newspapers for close to two decades, and is the editor of the hugely successful anthology, *Bomoicar: Stories of Bombay Goans, 1930–1980* (Goa 1556, 2014). She has spent five years in the development sector, documenting work for NGOs in education, health, human trafficking and related issues. She is currently enjoying a sabbatical.

Once Upon a Christmas

REENA MARTINS

As a boy in the 1940s, John Menezes came home from Christmas midnight mass at St. Xavier's Church in Poona, to an array of sweets. But what really stands out for John, is his Karachi granny's milk punch.

'The recipe, a British one, was eventually stolen, but I remember she'd let a concoction of rum, brandy, milk, lime and sugar stand for three weeks, strain and can it in a way that allowed air to escape. The curd in the residue then went into the tartlet crusts,' John said. The well-heeled Menezes family (their bungalow on the leafy Wellesley Road was rented from the father of industrialist, Azim Premji) was one of the few Goans at the time to own an oven. It was a British made Belling which baked the Christmas fruitcake and New Year's *bebinca*. But cakes were hardly regular fare in traditional Goan homes in the 1960s and '70s. The few households that did bake took their batters to neighbourhood bakeries.

Our family's *batega* (pronounced in Goa as *batk* [coconut cake]) and the little ribbon cake were baked in the blazing ovens of Persian Bakery in Poona's Kolsa Galli, the blacksmith's hub. But while the coconut in the *batega* on the aluminium platter survived the savage heat and the cake came out a beautiful golden brown, the ribbon cake bore deep scars. I'd watch in awe as my mother gently mixed the buttery yellow cake batter, swirling with pink and green in an enamel bowl — mum loved the starkness — but could never figure out how the batter that had nearly melted off my fingers, had turned bone dry when baked.

A few homes, like that of Marissa Sequeira[3] in Shirley Rajan village in Bandra, had a local contraption called the round oven, with sand in the centre. But in the 1960s, Marissa's maternal granny, Milagrinha D'Souza would walk in the biting cold with a stuffed piglet on a platter, from their home on 151, Hill Road, opposite New Talkies, to the bakery on Bandra's Bazar Road.

Marissa said, 'It had to be baked very early or the bakery could lose its vegetarian customers.'

At lunch, the carved suckling was served with sorpotel and vindalho, slow cooked on the coal stove.

Well-thumbed recipe books were dug out for the Christmas meal. For Ezilda Fernandes, a wedding dressmaker in Dhobi Talao, it was Pedro Damio Dias's *The Goan Cook's Guide* published c.1937, bought from BX Furtado's next door, that was the old faithful.

My mother, on the other hand, went by pure instinct when it came to her finger-licking sorpotel. It was the boiled meat that we'd lust after most, pinching it off the chopping board before it was sautéed with a dark and mysterious vinegary masala. Others like Eulogio Barretto in Byculla ate it religiously from Christmas Eve right through the season.

'My parents welcomed anyone in need of a meal,' said his daughter, Walesa.

When it came to traditional sweets, it always began with a cross at our home. Not the old rugged wooden cross but one still destined for the fire. Mum would pinch a tiny piece off the smooth hunk of dough and pull it roughly into shape with her expert hands. Once the dark glistening wok, up to its eyeballs with oil, was hot enough, mum, perched on the tiny wooden stool near the door of our little home in Pune, would quietly slip in the cross.

The tiny bronzy Pumix stove — quite a gun throat — was pulled off the shelf and from under its shroud to make the

---

3. Marissa Sequeira now lives in Atlanta, USA.

Christmas sweets. It was still the 1970s, and you had to wait a fortnight to get the gas cylinder you'd booked at the Hindustan Petroleum office. So kerosene from the ration shop always came to the rescue.

After dinner, our neighbours, Domacian uncle and his demure wife, Anna, would squat with us on the grass mat and roll out *neureos,* slide *cormollans* off the back of a fork and pinch *kulkuls* into dainty parcels.

Cynthia Gomes James[4] remembered her younger neighbours in Mazagon, shaping dough balls to make *neureos.* While the older ones rolled out the pastry, the 'experts' filled and sealed the *neureos* (pastry stuffed with sweetened coconut). The lady of the house then skilfully deep fried them.

Cynthia said, 'The sweets were put away in large tins and not touched till Christmas day.'

Not far off, at Khilchi Terrace, one of Grant Road's Dias Buildings, where afternoons are still redolent with the aroma of *mawa* cakes wafting in from the kitchen of the iconic B. Merwan's, neighbours were family. The four families on the fourth floor — one Mangalorean and three Goan, all thick as thieves — would huddle together after dinner, in the open-to-sky verandah.

'If we made *kulkuls* for aunty Carmen today, it was aunty Maria's turn tomorrow. It was so much fun and even the Muslim children from upstairs would join us,' said my aunt, Villa D'Souza, a grandmother of four, who spent nearly five happy decades raising a family in their Grant Road home.

It was a time of camaraderie. Nicknames drew hardly any offence. Our painter at Christmastime was know as 'Dammit' and till today none of us know his real name.

'If Daddy had to point out a flaw in the shade of paint, he'd go, "Dammit!" and so the name stuck,' my sister, Velma, told me.

---

4. Cynthia Gomes James now lives in Texas, USA.

Khoddo (baldy) was our Goan tailor who'd come over to stitch our
Christmas clothes — pencil tucked behind the ear — and amuse us
with terms like chicken and mutton sleeves. Ditto with *kaan kathro*
(ears cut), who was Marissa's family tailor.

Marissa said, 'He'd smoke hand-rolled *beedies* from the leaves of
a tree in our village, so we'd collect them for him.'

But the tree that stole the show was the live Christmas tree,
which was carried up from the garden to their first-floor house. It
was decorated with pretty ornaments from England, brought by
relatives from her mother, Mary's side. Mary D'Souza is India's first
female Olympian.

While Bandra's erstwhile fishing villages were dressed to the
nines, the hoi polloi in the Goan neighbourhoods in Byculla,
Mazagon, Grant Road and Dhobi Talao had their own stars to hang
outside. Almost every building with a sizeable Catholic population
produced a large star made from reeds and fine tissue paper. The
anticipation over them would even rival Sandra's eagerly awaited
halter dress or Marina's patent leather shoes.

Cynthia Gomes said, 'The group responsible for making them
would have their name, like Naka Boys or Durango Kids, displayed
on the star or on a banner.'

Back home from midnight Mass, the white, butter paper and
bamboo star was immediately turned on as we'd rush into the
waiting warmth of home. When the lights were put out, the deep-
red crib light, just above the cosy manger and the fairy lights on the
crib's roof stayed on. The silver, gold, red and green bunting stuck
from wall to wall, glowed in the dark.

Early next morning, a two-man band playing off-key tunes
on trumpets would wake us up. But till then, it would be a very
silent night.

John Lawrence Nazareth was educated at the University of Cambridge (Trinity College) and the University of California at Berkeley. He is a mathematical and algorithmic scientist, industry consultant, a university professor by vocation and an avocational travel and memoir writer, poet, essayist, and playwright. He makes his home on Bainbridge Island near Seattle, Washington, USA. Nazareth was born during the post-war years in Nairobi, Kenya, the son of J. Maximian Nazareth and Monica Freitas. His father was a prominent lawyer, nationalist, one-time president of the East Africa Indian National Congress, an elected member of the Kenya Legislative Council, and appointed Queen's Council in colonial Kenya. His grandfather, J.A. Nazareth, together with his granduncle, R.A. Nazareth, operated as the Nazareth Bros., and were hugely successful retailers, contributing much to the founding of Nairobi between 1899 and 1910. In his two memoirs *A Passage to Kenya* (2017) and *Up and About in Nairobi and Bombay* (2018), Nazareth recalls his life and that of his extended family in Africa and Bombay.

Young Under the Apple Boughs

JOHN LAWRENCE NAZARETH

Recollections from my childhood and early youth seem to have no definite timeline. Instead, they have coalesced into individual pools of memory and are ringed with golden auras that stand out against the dark, deep background of all that has been forgotten.

My earliest recollection is that of being seated on a hardwood floor and peering down into a darkened hole in a floorboard when I was little more than a year old. It is more a presence, or should I say a pre-sense, a memory of something that may not have happened. For me, however, it is real, my sole link to the 'wood-and-iron' house of my birth — wood because that was the material of its construction and iron because its roof was made from corrugated sheets of that metal. Shortly before my second birthday, my parents were fortunate enough to be able to move to a small stone bungalow about half a mile down the road, away from this wood-and-iron house in which they had lived in the first years of their marriage along with my father's unmarried sister, the widow of my father's eldest brother and her children, and at one time or another, two other brothers, one of them newly married. Houses were scarce in the years immediately following World War II. The wood-and-iron house has long since disappeared though I remember walking past a similar structure as a child, with my younger sister and brother, on our way to church.

The stone bungalow was rented from my father's eldest sister, Natividade, who had built it for her elder son. She was a large, slow-moving woman, soft and infinitely weary, who lived in the house immediately adjacent, within the same compound. My younger sister and brother were born in that bungalow. Like its more impressive neighbour, it is now in a sad state of disrepair.

Of my brother's birth, I retain another of those pools of memory: being placed next door in the care of Aunty Nathu and assured that the baby was soon to be dropped from an airplane. The traditional stork would surely have been simpler and less dangerous but I clearly remember that it was an airplane. I recall looking upwards anxiously at the sky, fearful of missing the moment of landing.

I lived my childhood, up to the age of twelve, in that house on Forest Road, and the memory of those years is best captured for me by 'Fern Hill', a poem by Dylan Thomas:

'When I was young and easy under the apple boughs
About the lilting house and happy as the grass was green'

Those for me were the apple days, my princedom my aunt's large compound within which our bungalow was located behind a tall kai-apple hedge — a plant of South African origin with little apricot-like fruit that ripen from hard green to soft golden yellow. It grew along the unpaved path for non-motorized traffic — pedestrians, bicyclists, and the occasional rider on horseback — that bordered Forest Road and demarcated the front boundary of the compound.

Forest Road took its name from a narrow fringe of forest, varying from one to three miles in width, which once grew on this land. A chronicler of early pioneering days, Errol Trzebinski, described this strip of forest as 'impenetrable' and 'magnificent', a place where animals followed secret paths and visitors were entranced by the foliage, butterflies and flowers. But as Nairobi grew progressively, from a railway station and frontier town into the capital city of a newly-established colony, the forested fringe had given way to segregated, residential suburbs; for example, Parklands and Muthaiga, where only immigrants of European origin were permitted to live. The flora and fauna receded into smaller, isolated forest preserves or into the vast, mysterious, and dangerously lonely stretch of forested land known as the Nairobi City Park. This park lay immediately beyond the sports fields of the Indian community, in particular, the Patel Club and the Sikh Union, which bordered Forest Road to the north, while along the entire length of this road to the south, within gated compounds, were the homes of families of Indian origin — Hindus, Muslims, Sikhs, Parsis, Goans — comprising another segregated, residential suburb of the city. Aunty Nathu's was one of these compounds, and it had retained a little of the magic of that earlier pre-colonial time. Within its hedged boundaries grew a large variety of trees and shrubs, many of them fruit or vegetable-bearing, which had been planted by an unknown hand to replace the indigenous forest. It was a garden of delights, enormous in the eyes of a child. And, whilst the wild animals of the forest had long retreated into the confines of the Nairobi National Park, on the southern outskirts of the city, or to the open Athi plains beyond, the butterflies and birds of the forest had remained.

Despite the passage of time, I can reconstruct with precision the layout of the grounds. Between the two houses grew the centrepiece of the compound, a huge mango tree with branches that spread over our red, corrugated-iron roof and bore plentiful fruit in season. As a child, I loved to clamber up into its lower limbs to pick a semi-ripe mango, which is delicious when sliced around the large seed and the flesh laced with a sprinkling of chili-powder and salt. This area between the two houses was a mini-orchard in itself, containing a pomegranate tree, alongside a spreading fig bush that yielded fruit, which turned from green to dark purple. And beside it grew a little banana grove.

Next to our front bedroom window was a spreading mulberry bush, and behind the house, a tall mulberry tree. In season, it carpeted the ground beneath with furry, deep-purple berries. A sweet potato patch spread wild, covering a wide area behind this mulberry tree. This was an especially joyful place for me, because within the foliage were to be found ladybirds, insects smaller than a child's finger nail, spotted and polished like brightly coloured beads, most commonly red or orange with little black spots. Most often they would fly off when I tried to capture them in my enclosed palm, but sometimes I was successful, once even succeeding in imprisoning a little collection in a matchbox. I was told that these pretty little creatures could crawl into the ears when you were asleep, and, on that pretext, my six-year old sister, Jeanne, took it upon herself to release back into the garden this precious collection. In the ensuing uproar, Njoroge, our Kikuyu cook was dispatched to the sweet potato patch to gather replacements, my protests silenced, and my sister suitably admonished despite the dangers she had supposedly protected us from.

A well-trodden footpath demarcated the boundary of the sweet potato patch and it led from our back door to Njoroge's living quarters at the rear of the compound. In addition to skills in cooking and capturing ladybirds, Njoroge was very adept at removing jiggers, nasty little members of the flea family that lived in the black cotton soil of the compound. We children were cautioned never to go out in the compound in bare feet, because one ran the risk of a female jigger burrowing into the exposed skin and taking up residence to lay her eggs. Left unattended, this wound would fester and ultimately even turn gangrenous. So a jigger had to be removed promptly and carefully using a needle, whose pointed end was first sterilized with a burning match. Less threatening creatures called antlions also inhabited the black cotton soil and they fascinated me greatly. Their burrows were marked by little inverted cones of very finely sifted soil. If one took a twig and carefully worked it round and round within the fine grains of soil, one might unearth one of these little creatures before it could burrow deeper. I'd spend happy hours in search of them.

A little lemon tree grew within the sweet potato patch and on the other side of the path, about twenty or thirty yards from our back door, was a lemon-orange tree, the result of a cutting from a lemon tree being grafted onto the root stock of an orange tree, or perhaps it was the other way around, yielding a hybrid that bore both types of fruit on its two main stems. And next to this hybrid was another large mango tree, somewhat smaller than the one between the two houses and nowhere as productive.

The lemon-orange hybrid, however, retains a sad pool of memory for me. One morning, when the sleep had barely fallen from my eyes, I wandered down the L-shaped passageway that led from the bedroom shared with my two siblings, still dressed in my pyjamas and with my catapult in hand. Looking out the back door, over the couple of small steps that led down to the backyard of the house, I spotted a movement in this far off lemon-orange tree and without aiming at anything in particular I fired off a shot in its direction. To my surprise, out dropped a little red robin, stone dead! These tiny birds, which have a deep red breast and a brownish back and wings, weigh less than an ounce and are much smaller than their American counterparts, which also happen to be called robins. (The latter are longer and leaner looking, generally have orange breasts and greyish wings and are at least twice the size and weight.)

By some unfortunate accident of fate, this little red robin had perched on a branch within this tree, directly in the line of fire. But, instead of delight at my unexpected success, my reaction, when I picked up the lifeless little creature from where it had fallen to the ground, was to be heart stricken. I was overcome with sadness, and, thereafter, I lost interest in my catapult. The reason why hunters and fishermen find pleasure in tormenting and killing living, breathing creatures remains a mystery to me to this day. I can recall another unexpected encounter, but this time rewarding, in the backyard of the compound. One morning, a huge tortoise appeared, seemingly out of nowhere. It must have crawled out of the Nairobi City Park and through the playing fields, crossed Forest Road at night when the traffic was minimal, and then into our compound. It stayed for a few days and then it was gone. A silent visitor from an alien world!

Fatima M. Noronha writes stories and edits books. Over the last 45 years, a few hundred of her short pieces — articles, reflections, fiction and memoir — have featured in regional, national and overseas print publications, and occasionally on air or online. Goa 1556 published *Stray Mango Branches* (2013), a collection of vignettes of Goan life. She won the *Joao Roque Literary Journal's* Best in Non-fiction Award 2017 for her piece 'The Menino Will Come Tonight.' Born in Lisbon, she moved to Goa with her parental family in the 1960s and later gypsied around India with her fighter pilot husband and their two daughters — Fatima has called many places home. In her stories she shares with the reader the places and people she collected in her heart. She now lives in Goa, and carries her grandson around the garden where she grows a little fruit for her family and a good deal for the koels and babblers in the vicinity.

The Menino Will Come Tonight

FATIMA M. NORONHA

Lisbon, 24 December, 1962

A woman sits sewing by candlelight, which throws a warm glow on her fair face. Rembrandt? Millet? McGregor? Timeless in a time well remembered, my mother sits sewing near the one candle in the room.

The picture, a hiccup in modernity, remains with me. Our years of working by candlelight in Goa would come later. Born in Lisbon, and never having travelled far from it, that was the first power failure I ever saw. I did not know it, but the coldest European winter since 1740 had just begun. Christmas Eve, not St. Agnes's, but *ah, bitter chill it was!*

Mamã is hemming a mint-green woollen dress she tailored, treadling her trusty Singer in spurts last week, a low-waisted dress with two green bows on the belt. Only the wearer will know the secret: behind the belt are hidden pockets. Two pockets, what more can a dress offer?! It is my Christmas dress, or maybe Noémia's: Mamã always makes us clothes which are identical except for the sizes. I am twice as old as my sister and therefore taller, though she is plump and I am skinny.

It is Monday, and we are all on vacation. Even my parents have four days off. So it is quite unusual that Mamã has not yet finished sewing our dresses, which we shall wear tonight to midnight Mass. She likes to be ahead of time. But, of course, she has been busy making fruit cake, filling the house with the scent of burning caramel which she stirs with a long, narrow spoon in the *fervedor,* the one-handled one-litre boiler. Des and I help to deseed the sultanas, and then we get a fistful as payment. His fist is bigger than mine because he is eight. In any case, he is Mamã's pet and gets a little more, but I don't mind. After midnight Mass we shall eat all the cake we want, along with our yearly tot of port.

Everyone has been busy today. Oscar, our grown-up cousin who lives with us, made the crib. On the kitchen floor, right up to where Mamã and the strong ladies chop and stir and wash, he spread out big sheets of brown paper. Then he dipped an old sock in green paint and quickly made a mess of all the papers. Another sock went into red paint and another into yellow. He hung out the papers to dry on the long clothesline near the row of windows. All the windows in the house are closed these days because of Mamã's greatest enemy, the draught. But — would you believe it? — there was sunshine all morning in the row of kitchen windows. There are no curtains on that side, which is all glass from the sill to the ceiling, but the glass is thick and knobbly so you can't see clearly through. When the painted papers were almost dry, Oscar crumpled them and made them into the hills of Bethlehem, with a cave for the animals and Mother Mary and Joseph. The *Menino* will come tonight.

By tea-time it is already night and there are no lights. We knew the lights would not come on when we pressed the switch, because Mamã's neat little room heater has been a cold metal box for a while now. She calls out to the strong ladies. Maria do Rosário and Maria Amélia Gorda (fat), who weighs a hundred kilos, have lived with us for years, but we love Rosário more because she tells us such crazy stories while we eat, and she is great fun. When Mamã calls, Rosário says, *'Minha senhora?'* and comes running in from the kitchen, and then I go with her back to the kitchen and we pull out the sink drawer and stir the paper bags and bottle openers and rolls of string till we find a candle and a matchbox, and come back here to the foyer — the *sala* is closed till midnight.

There were other times we children were not allowed into the parlour. The doorway of the *sala* is one of my early memories. 1959? 1960? We wanted to see what was happening in there, but the door would open only a crack because a very big instrument — a double-bass as I saw it but more likely a cello — was very near it. The room was full of runaway Goans, mostly men in their twenties, all of them talented musicians, including Fortunato and Salvador Figueiredo, and the later famous pianist Noel Flores. They were rehearsing *Sonsar Charuch-re Disancho* for a recording.

There were many such rehearsals. Those were warm, even stuffy, evenings, nothing like this Christmas Eve.

✳

Except for my father, who cannot sit for long — he is the one who struck the match and lit the candle, he is the one who lit that monster of a kerosene radiator which hisses and hums in the corridor — all of us are sitting around Mamã, not around the radiator: Desmond, Noémia, Oscar, Maria Amélia, Maria do Rosário and I. Every little while, Dadá pulls back the beige curtains and looks out of the French windows at small skies on both sides of the unlit building across Rua Conde de Sabugosa. Though we live on the sixth floor, under the clouds, we can only see the big sky when we are out on our terrace, where we play *futebol* and Rosário makes sure we stay away from the railing. Till April, Mamã will not let us step onto the terrace. She fears we might catch our death of cold.

✳

For Des and me, that was the last Christmas of our childhood, we with our parents, all of us warm together in that coldest winter. The very next Christmas my father would spend alone in that house, unable to bring himself to listen to our recorded messages and carols. We would not spend Christmas together until 1968 in Goa, and our way to Goa was long and winding.

1961 had sorted my parents, and us children with them, into the box marked enemies of Goa. But Goa was where they had planned to live eventually. Meanwhile, my mother had not seen her parents in Bombay for many years, nor had they seen their daughter's progeny, except for Des as a baby. In the summer of 1963, my parents went to London to do the paperwork, as Lisbon and Delhi were not on talking terms. Our livid Mamã was obliged to apply to a British officer, as she said, 'for a visa to enter my own country.' Leaving our Dadá in Lisbon in December that year, the four of us boarded a returning chartered plane which had ferried a payload of Goans from Karachi to Lisbon. The visa did not come in time for Christmas in Bombay, so we spent it in Karachi at the home of Mamã's sister Leah and her husband Patrick. 'Mamã!' bleated Uncle Pat, imitating us. There was little we could say in reply, since we spoke only Portuguese. For Des, Noémia and me, Pakistan was our first taste of India.

But Christmas night 1962 we were still together and Lisboa was home. Downtown, in the Praça do Rossio, the flower vendors — peasant women in scarves and thick black shawls — lit a fire on the cobbles to survive that midnight when business was certain, despite the weather. It just got colder and colder until it was a fraction of a degree from zero. Zero in Lisbon, can you imagine? But it did not rain, so we went dry-shod to midnight Mass. My parents never owned a car, and we were possibly born walking, but as long as we lived in Lisbon we went to Mass in a Merc. Lisbon taxis were made by Mercedes Benz — still are.

We lived in a northern suburb where everything was available — open spaces for evening walks, parks with swings, schools, markets, an airport, and two modern churches to choose from. For

impractical reasons of their own, maybe to pretend they were home
in Goa at Christmas, for midnight Mass our parents opted to take us
right across the city, almost down to the Tagus *(o Tejo, o Tejo!),* to the
Baroque Igreja de São Roque, the earliest Jesuit church in Portuguese
territory, a tough old pile which survived the earthquake of 1755.
Plain on the outside, its interior is said to be the most beautiful of
any church in Portugal. It is certainly more highly decorated than a
field marshal. There is a special chapel there dedicated to St. Francis
Xavier, a favourite saint in Goa. Every year, on the 3rd of December,
homesick Goans in Lisbon would organise a Mass at São Roque, so
it was there that I first heard that most Goan of all Konkani hymns,
San Franciscu Xaviera, sung forth with ardour and punctuated with
sniffles. My father's eyes would moisten too, and I would wonder
what the fuss was about. He was not shy, but he did not tell us his
grandfather Raimundo composed the hymn.

Christmas Eve 1962, at night, wearing our new outfits and old
overcoats, we were packed into a Mercedes. We three children sat on
three adult laps, and Des favoured an adult in a window seat. He got
to look out, and also to make free with a whole frosted windowpane,
etching hearts and crossing them out, *coração, rabiscos,* heart, squiggles.
We loved the night ride, but somewhat less than a daytime one. We
reached São Roque just before midnight, in time to hear a children's
choir sing *Vinde, Jesus Menino,* Come, Little Boy Jesus!

Christmas in Council Time — linking the Council's keynote
hope to the Christmas hope — was the message Lisbon's new
Cardinal, José da Costa Nunes, broadcast that night. Two months
earlier, in Rome, the Second Vatican Council had begun. It is
possible the preacher at Igreja de São Roque mentioned something
of the sort too, but I have no mental record. My eyes followed the
dull floorboards (so unlike the parquetry of our humble abode
which Maria do Rosário waxed and polished to mirror point)
between our pew and the next, and the strange old railing along the
side aisle, and the flickering candles. Then they closed.

We were all wide awake when we reached home after midnight Mass. The familiar ceremony in the parlour, which had been out of bounds to us children all that day, was the high point of our *feliz Natal.* In the corner nearest the window, Dadá and Oscar had set up a beautiful Nativity scene, and a Christmas tree, and below the tree were heaps of presents — Dadá never did things by halves. Among the toys he had bought for Noémia was a yellow duck too large to be wrapped. Portuguese toys were works of art. That *pato* was the only open gift, so we all saw it right away, and my sister could not take her eyes off it. The rule was that we first sang *Adeste Fideles* and kissed the toes of the baby in the manger, and only then could we open our presents. It therefore went like this:

All (in solemn unison): *Adeste fideles, laeti triumphantes …*
Noémia (breathless): *Um pato!*
All (grinning in unison): *Venite, venite in Bethlehem!*

TRAVELOGUES

Jessica Faleiro (see bio on page 18)

A Goan in Macau

JESSICA FALEIRO

In *Sun After Dark,* Pico Iyer writes, 'The modern, shifting world has
brought disorientation home to us, and mystery and strangeness;
even in the most familiar places we may come upon something
unsettling ...' As I walk through the streets of modernised Macau,
I recall these lines from one of my favourite travel writers, and
I realise that I am confronted with the opposite. This Special
Administrated Region (SAR) of China was administered by
Portugal from the mid-1500s to 1999, after which it was 'handed
back' to the Chinese government. All around me, I can hear what I
guess is Cantonese, but every now and then, a Portuguese word or
two drifts to my ears and I turn around in search of the speaker, in
vain. It seems as if familiar ghosts of the past are haunting me in
this remote Far East Asian territory.

I was born on the west coast of India, in Goa; a state which,
like Macau, was also under Portuguese rule for over four centuries.
The few Goans I've spoken to about Macau have nostalgic notions
of an ex-colonial sister-seaport. Macau, like Goa, had a diverse
population of missionaries, businessmen and soldiers moving
through its port. Similarly, locals took on Portuguese influences
that are imprinted in Macanese architecture, culture and food. Like
fraternal twins, Goa and Macau have similar interiors with different
outward appearances. For example, take Goa's Latin Quarter,
Fontainhas, where the street signs are blue lettering on white tile.
But here, although it's the same mock-azulejos design, the signs

are in Cantonese and Portuguese — the two languages that locals communicate in. Macau's churches, protected by UNESCO World Heritage status, remind me of Old Goa's similarly preserved clutch of ecclesiastical buildings.

I've been invited to participate in Macau's two-week long annual literary festival, The Script Road. I'm staying for only six days and the schedule is jam-packed with interviews, panel events and writing workshops. In the time in between, when I can fit in some sightseeing, I'm determined to discover whatever I can of the city's tangible links to Goa and India, and the first diamond in the rough I begin hunting for is the Moorish Barracks.

Walking up a steep slope, I see the sharp corner of an elevated building jutting out into the street. Built in 1874, the brick and stone, neo-classical edifice was constructed to accommodate an Indian regiment from Goa appointed to reinforce Macau's police force. It forms a reminder of the close links forged between Goa, as Portugal's administrative seat in the East, and its Far Eastern ex-colony of Macau, dangling off one end of China. The pristine yellow and white building with wide verandahs, stands on a raised granite platform, towering above street level with direct views of the riverside, allowing authorities to monitor the flow of boats in and out of the Inner Harbour. It now functions as the headquarters of Macau's Harbour Authority and I'm a little intimidated by the security guard posted outside, so I stop myself from taking a closer look.

Though there isn't time to visit it, later, I find out that the Punjabi and Gujarati Muslims in the Indian regiment from Goa were buried in a cemetery called 'Ramal dos Mouros' or 'Extension of the Moors.' The Lusophone world referred to people who followed the Islamic culture as Moors, associating them with the 7th century Muslim inhabitants that once lived in what is now Morocco, Spain and Portugal.

Apart from an occasional tourist and a few local Chinese milling about on errands, the back streets and alleyways away from the city centre are uncannily quiet. I come across lots of small mom-and-pop eateries selling local specialties out of small spaces that seem like garages kitted out with tiny make-shift kitchens, and a couple of circular tables for communal eating. But most of them are empty. I spot a lone man placing a rather large offering of some sort in front of a little pavement altar wedged between two shop-fronts. On closer inspection, I notice it's a cooked chicken, head included. The grotesque offering is unfamiliar, even though the concept of the altar is not; every Goan Hindu and Catholic household I know has one.

My first introduction to the city aside, I rush to the Old Court building, a dull, cement-grey erection with neo-classical columns, built in 1951 on Avenida da Praia Grande, where they're hosting the literary festival. I'm just in time for an interview with *Tribuna Macau Journal* and a twenty-minute photo session with the festival's photographer, Eduardo Martins. Perhaps, he notices jet-lag setting in and takes pity on me, or maybe he just wants to ensure I take a high-energy photo, but he keeps me in seamless conversation, interjecting only briefly to ask me to strike a pose in profile or to stand behind a chair. He tells me that besides the Chinese and the Macanese, the Portuguese make up a good percentage of the population here and most of them are journalists, in advertising or lawyers. I learn that one of the conditions of handing Macau back to China was that Portuguese laws would continue to be upheld for fifty more years or so, there are a sizeable number of Portuguese lawyers living in Macau who are still needed to interpret and enforce existing legislation.

The population of Macau is about half a million people, of which only about 20,000 are native Macanese of mixed Chinese, Portuguese and Malay heritage, though the numbers vary depending on who you speak to. The Macanese population is notoriously close-knit and I'm told that they tend to mix only among themselves, though many of them have settled abroad. Over 90 percent of Macau's population is Chinese and about five percent is Portuguese. I wonder what this means to the minority population of Macanese still living on this little strip of land that, in 1557, was handed over to the Portuguese by the Ming Court, in exchange for getting rid of the pirate stronghold that was a major problem for Chinese shipping then.

As I'm about to leave the building I meet Helder Beja, director of The Script Road, for the first time face-to-face. I thank him for the invitation and am pleased to learn that I'm the first Goan author they've had at the festival since its inception in 2012.

I wake up the next day to a wet and gloomy spring morning. 'It's typical for Macau at this time of the year while we're transitioning into summer,' I'm told by the cheerful Filipino hotel concierge. I have an interview with Marco Carvalho, the thick-bearded editor-in-chief of *Ponto Final,* Macau's main Portuguese broadsheet and sponsor of The Script Road. He asks whether I feel rootless, having grown up outside of Goa for most of my life, and tries to tease out how much being of Goan origin relates to my sense of identity. It's after he's switched off his voice recorder and we slip into a casual chat about Macau's links to India that Marco tells me about a lesser-known sub-community of Macanese from Daman, Gujarat, living in Macau. Considering the number of ethnicities from the Malay Peninsula, Hong Kong, Portugal, Goa and even Russia that have been integrated into Macau over the years, it is no surprise to find a Gujarati community settled here as well.

Hardly surprising then, that the Macanese people are going through an identity crisis, exacerbated by the influx of mainland Chinese into the tiny territory over the last twenty years or so. Another Portuguese expat, Claudia, tells me that the Macanese once spoke Patois, a Portuguese-root Creole language of their own, which has all but disappeared, and I wonder if any of them feel alienated in their own home.

Claudia adds, 'Although the imprint of the Portuguese may still subsist in the city, Macanese culture seems destined to disappear, diluted in a sea of mainland Chinese. I think you can see that sadness in the old Macanese people's eyes.'

Later, on a panel with noted Australian novelist, Brian Castro, we discuss how the question of identity enters our work. I talk about my experience of being a Third Culture Kid, with Goan parents, who has spent the majority of her childhood and working life outside of Goa, and how it helps define one's identity, through their humanity, rather than by politicized boundaries. Immediately after, I'm taken aside for a live interview by Radio Macau's engaging broadcaster, Karlos, who asks me to elaborate on the idea of Third Culture Kids. As I answer, I'm impressed by his ability to seamlessly move between translating what I'm saying into Portuguese for the live show and back again to question me in English. Afterwards, Karlos and I end up having a lengthy conversation about how my global mobility helps me perceive the challenges behind global political movements unfolding in the world today. He shares with me how amazed he was to discover so many ethnicities in Macau when he first arrived here a few years ago.

There's a treat in store for a group of us at the Institute of Tourism Studies where I've been invited to lunch, served by their catering students, before delivering a talk about travel writing to 200 students. I've ordered the Macanese dish Galinha Africana, which has a spicy, satay sauce and is served on a bed of couscous with kalamat olives and raisins. It's savoury tang is unlike any Goan or Portuguese dish I've tasted. The chef tells us that the recipe has Mocambiquan and Goan influences found in the spice rub marinade and the sauce. I top off the meal with a dessert trio of mango soufflé, egg custard and a mini-Serradurra or 'Sawdust pudding.' The last is a delightful dish that one can find in Goan homes. As I spoon mouth-watering morsels of cream and crunch into my mouth, I feel that ghost of the ever-familiar lingering in the air.

I know I cannot leave Macau without seeing its emblematic postcard icon, the towering façade of the 'Ruins of St. Paul' on Largo da Companhia de Jesus. The façade is all that remains of the 17th century church complex that caught fire and was almost completely destroyed during a typhoon in 1835. The ruins sit atop a hill with 68 stone steps leading up to it. Through the entrance and just underneath the church is the Museum of Sacred Art; a small room of religious ornaments and artefacts. The provenance of each item seems to be based largely on guesswork as most items have vague labels. But, a few objects catch my eye, like the life-size, painted wood statue of St. Augustine that is labelled, 'Indo-Portuguese work, 17th century.' That familiar haunting makes me choose to read it as 'Made in Goa.'

To one side of the inner complex is an excavated area entitled the St. Francis Xavier Chapel. The little plaque next to it doesn't offer much information. Later, I find out that Coloane, a drive south of the city centre, has a chapel built in 1928 dedicated to St. Francis Xavier, which, supposedly, once contained bone fragments of his fingers and rosary beads that belonged to him.

St. Francis Xavier died on the island of San Chuan, located about 70 km to the west of Macau, while he was on a mission to Japan. His miraculous body, which was found to be intact and uncorrupted when exhumed from his initial internment, was eventually brought to Old Goa where it remains today, entombed in a glass and silver casket. This and the other strong, tangible, lasting connections to Goa make me wonder what other kinds of connections Goa and Macau might have.

I've heard that there are opium traders buried in a cemetery in Macau; I wonder if they have a Goa connection. Panjim was built around the 1820s with revenues arising from the Portuguese opium trade. Macau was a location known to facilitate the movement of opium around Asia. What else could caravels have left behind in Macau from Goa, besides spices, that isn't recorded in some artefact or document? Pirates were reported to have lived and operated out of Macau up until the 1920s. What if a pirate or two were originally from Goa, or even better, an ancestor of mine!

The writer in me is entranced by the myriad of possible stories that lie around every corner and within every person I meet. The evening before I leave, I have to remind myself that I've been so steeped in unfurling the secrets buried within Macau's layers that I've completely forgotten to take a look inside one of the casinos that define modern Macau.

Legalised gambling in Macau dates back to when Chinese gambling dens started paying rent to the government under a licensing system. Since the handover in 1999, there are over 30 established casinos in Macau, many of which are established names in Las Vegas like Wynn, Galaxy and Sands. The soulless-ness of these massive structures pervasively drains all energy, spirit and character away from their surroundings and swallows them into a black hole sourced from their gambling pits. The casinos account for 50 percent of the economy, so I suppose the locals have to find a way to make their peace with this traumatic rent in their skyline, punctuated by glitzy neon monstrosities like the Grand Lisboa, a giant steel and glass thistle-shaped structure shooting upwards from the ground.

It's a brief, free shuttle bus-ride to The Venetian from my hotel, so I escape for two hours to see what all the fuss is about. The sheer extravagance, opulence and superficiality of Macau's largest casino, complete with an uncannily real indoor-sky and fake lagoon with Venetian gondolas, is something you have to walk around in, in order to fully comprehend. It's a space that largely sets the tone for the Macau I've seen so far — a handful of heritage sites that have been preserved for commercial tourism, while the rest have been destroyed to make way for modern development that reflect nothing of Macau's rich and diverse cultural heritage.

There's almost no sign left of the fishing villages that once characterised the coastal edge, except in parts of Coloane and Taipa. The churches have been renovated, but the farther you move away from the city centre, the more tawdry the buildings and narrow streets start to look. Apart from meeting a couple of Chinese-Macau residents who were born and brought up in the region, I've been interacting mostly with Portuguese and Filippino expats who are kind enough to share with me what little they know about the city that is their temporary home. But, underneath it all, I know there is more to Macau for those willing to stay still and uncover what lies beneath. Considering that I came to Macau without any sense of nostalgia weighing me down, or any expectations of wanting to stay longer than six days to participate in The Script Road, I find myself unusually drawn to Macau. I hope to return again, so that I can continue to unearth the familiar lodged in the unfamiliar.

R. Benedito Ferrão has lived and worked in Kuwait, India, the United States, England and Australia. A writer and academic, he is currently an Assistant Professor of English and Asian & Pacific Islander American Studies at the College of William and Mary. In 2017–18, he curated the art exhibition *Goa/Portugal/Mozambique: The Many Lives of Vamona Navelcar* (Fundação Oriente Gallery, Goa), and edited a book of the same title to accompany this retrospective of Navelcar's art. His fiction and non-fiction appear in *Riksha, The Good Men Project, Mizna, India Currents,* and other publications. Sometimes mistaken for a celebrity chef of apparently similar mien, Ferrão hopes to parlay his 'fame' into a parallel career as a purveyor of truly awful meals for hipsters who cannot tell the difference.

Status: Unknowable

R. BENEDITO FERRÃO

'And how do you say your name?'

I am prepared for this question. 'Feh-AO,' I over-enunciate with great geniality. The official attempts to mimic the sound I've just made. 'Fer-OH?'

My name provides the finest bait-and-switch. In this moment, I am secretly grateful to the Portuguese for happening upon my people's shores some five hundred years ago and bestowing upon us their multi-syllabic monikers. (Never mind that de Albuquerque himself likely had the Moors to thank for his Arabic-sounding name and that he dethroned the Muslim king of our coast.) And they say colonialism gave us nothing!

'Don't worry,' I commiserate. 'I don't think I say it quite right myself.'

He smiles and waves me through.

Self-deprecation is a lost art. I sail through the checkpoint, name mangled, but passport restored.

I always check in online the day before the flight. Even if it's a domestic flight, I still take my American passport with me — all other forms of governmental identification are too whimsical for these endeavours. I must always resist the urge, nonetheless, to place said passport in a frame of gold that I would hold up like a monstrance on the Highest of High Holy days. The car service has been ordered to arrive a full fifteen minutes before I actually have to leave my home to get to the airport a full two hours before the time at which I'd have to board the flight (which is a full half-hour before the flight is actually scheduled to depart).

That same night, I will have packed all the things I will take on my trip in clear resealable bags. On Monday, I will have gone to the supermarket to replenish my store of these containment apparatus. I need them in small, medium, large, and pillowcase. Don't worry — I recycle. I reuse the bags as often as I can. I always take the same things and so I've learned to pack efficiently. At first, I place all the items that are to be sequestered upon the bed in a grid by degree of size. The socks can go into the smallest size bags if I fold them just right. The underwear in the medium. The shirts are stacked in pairs and fit neatly into the larger bags. The trousers will have to go into the largest. When these bags are close to disintegration, I will use them to hold the snacks I take to work. And when they truly cannot be used anymore, I'll place them in the blue recycling bin.

I know the TSA agent who will check my suitcase would appreciate my efforts to reduce, reuse, and renew, were I able to let him know how earth-conscious I am. I don't want him to worry about the multitudinous amounts of plastic he will see when he opens my suitcase. He will kindly let me know that he has randomly checked my luggage, by placing an advisory note lovingly on top of all these see-through packages. He will appreciate that I've made his job so much easier by letting him survey at one glance all that my valise holds, and that there is nothing suspicious about my possessions, even if he thinks that the person who has organized and contained these items must seek help for their neurosis. I shall add the informative note he will leave me about how these luggage checks are about my safety to the pile I have collected at home. They remind me of how secure I should feel after the completely routine and random check of my ziplocked underwear.

Also on Monday, I will have acquired new razor blades from the store. I need this to complete my pre-travel toilette. On the night preceding my departure, I will scan YouTube for the latest advice on how to shave so closely that my face will take on its once pre-pubescent mien. This is a challenge, you see, given that every pore on my face sprouts four hairs from each root. Warm wet towels, shave cream, brushes, razors, balms, aftershaves and unguents will be laid out on my vanity alongside my laptop. From this gadget, the media star I have chosen to counsel me on the occasion will expertly deliver step-by-step instructions on how to relieve myself of the hirsuteness of my face. But, just to be certain, I'll also shave against the grain. In the morning, I'll wake up an extra half hour before I normally would to repeat the process. The shaving industry loves my facially hairy race, no doubt. But let it be known that they, too, are doing their bit for national security with the inability of their razor blades to last beyond a few uses.

As an added precaution, I trim my eyebrows. They have betrayed me at the best of times, adding punctuation to my unvoiced thoughts on an otherwise expressionless (and hairless face). It's like they function independently of all my other facial features, operating heedlessly to reveal my otherwise so well repressed feelings. These damned arches will rise higher than Greek pillars of yore, and rival the sweep of the Arc de Triomphe. One simply cannot have this. Taming these shrewish brows will ensure some measure of control over their wantonness when my travel documents are requested and carefully pored over as if they are written in a language so long dead, it would take a doctorate-holding scholar to decipher their authenticity. But as I tell myself (and my querulous eye-framing pelts), this is indubitably in the service of making everyone's experience at the airport (and the nation at large) just that little bit better. Down, eyebrows, down!

At the gate, as I count down the time to my flight, I shall pull out the book that I always carry with me when I fly. Its title is innocuous, its cover non-descript, its content never actually consumed. The book is just a prop — it might as well be part of the carefully curated costume I always wear when flying. Let's start with my shoes. Non-marking soles, dark uppers, no metal parts. My slacks, also dark, comfortable, but most importantly button-flied. This is a necessary detail. Getting in and out of airplane bathrooms rapidly helps keep one's bodily functions from being misconstrued for other activities. For this reason, I will also not have consumed any liquids up to three hours prior to my flight. And certainly no diuretics. Coffee, tea, and alcohol will not know my insides for several hours. I absolutely appreciate that the cabin pressure and unusually cold air in the aircraft will drain any remaining moisture from my skin, so that upon arrival I shall bear the appearance of an unbandaged mummy. The premature aging this will result in is unfortunate, but the dehydration is tantamount to one less visit to the cloistered space of the bathroom in the sky. Indeed, those obscuring doors, that fold like origami to conceal one's whereabouts for a few minutes are evidently cause for concern. It is best to limit one's forays into these alcoves' mysterious depths.

But I digress. My travel trousers have never known the constriction of a belt. The metal buckles of such bondage devices are tricksters waiting to set off the scanners. It is true that I am often to be seen shimmying in airports as I try to pull my trousers back upon my buttocks. For this reason, I stay seated for as long as one can before the boarding process ensues.

Upon my torso will be seen no letters or patterns, for my t-shirt and its encasing jacket will be devoid of any such visual encumbrance. I don't want anyone to be of the impression that Nike might be the holy deity to which I profess my devotion and loyalty to such an unfettered extent that I would be willing to lay down my life for them.

This tried and tested ensemble is as practical as it is elegant while being, at the same time, completely inconspicuous. That I look like someone from an Old Navy commercial, circa 2003, 1999, and 2017, is a compliment I will take for my sartorial ability to be the very definition of a yawn-inducing suburbanite.

Occasionally, a fellow-passenger will attempt to engage me in conversation as we both await entry into the hallowed space of the metal bird. I am prepared.

'You on this flight?' they'll ask.

I'll look up from the book I am not reading, push back the glasses I do not need to read (but such a useful travel prop, I must say!), and smile.

'Uh huh!'

In those two syllables I will have successfully made known my friendliness, while also politely demonstrating that my communication skills are those of someone more given to rumination that utterance. The spectacles work well, too, to affect just that slight bit of nerdiness which everyone knows to be a sure sign of lovably excusable social ineptitude.

'Flight's late again!' someone else will proclaim within earshot and obviously with the intention of bringing me into a collective rant about the general nature of air travel today and how it no longer bears the charms and glamour of the golden era when one dressed up in their Sunday best to travel and were served martinis while discussing how the good ol' boys were doing in the playoffs. In response, I will let my eye catch theirs for the briefest of seconds, sigh, shoulders raised and lowered just so, smile, and then go back to not reading my book. I love being a friendly part of the community at the airport.

It is now that moment we have all been waiting for. We are about to board the flight. The bag I carry is the perfect size so that — you guessed it! — I can occupy my seat quickly after having stowed my luggage efficaciously and without incident. But then, alas! Disaster strikes.

'Ladies and gentlemen,' the flight attendant's garbled voice says over the PA. 'I must ask you to deplane.'

For this I am not prepared.

As I retrieve my bag and share unplanned eye contact with the other passengers who slowly make their way to the exit, I feel the sweat seep through my t-shirt, creating a pattern around my speedily beating heart and spelling out tell-tale words across my heaving chest. My trousers start a mutinous descent down my flanks. My decoy book looks even to me like a manual for mayhem. My heretofore empty bladder threatens to betray me at any moment, its contents brimming alarmingly.

Back at the holding pen after we make our egress, I feel the itch of someone staring at me. I pretend to pay rapt attention to the airline staff who are about to make an announcement.

'We're really sorry, folks. We'll have you back on the plane momentarily. Slight maintenance issue — one of the toilets needed to be unclogged.'

Don't look at me, dude. I didn't need to go to the bathroom until just now!

We are allowed back onto the plane. I take my seat by the window and anticipate the arrival of the person who will make the journey alongside me. When they show up, I am given not more than a look and am said nothing to, which suits me just fine. My practiced smile turns up the corners of my lips for a millisecond and I return to the ardent non-study of the tome in my hands. Only a few hours before this journey is done. It's so close at this point that I can taste it!

Closely shaven to within tasting distance of my circulatory system, properly packed with methods to unimpede security's optics, meticulously dehydrated to the point of being shrivelled up into a raisin, what I want more than anything is to have a drink. But I cannot afford such a luxury while the mission still remains unfulfilled! Exhaustion looms, but I am wired. I look like I am devouring every last letter in this well-thumbed book …

Not until I am off the plane, have retrieved my suitcase (I cannot wait to read the love-letter the TSA have left me this time), and departed the sanctum of the airport that I allow myself the pleasure of declaring victory. I have made it through without raising suspicion of my birth in the Middle East!

But I cannot let this triumph soften me. I must begin plotting for my return in a few days hence. Do I have enough re-sealable bags?

POETRY

Salil Chaturvedi's short fiction and poetry have appeared in various journals, including *Antiserious, Himal, Indian Quarterly, Indian Literature, Out of Print, Wasafiri, Guftugu, Indian Cultural Forum, The Sunflower Collective.* Comics and haiku are old loves. His haiku and haibun have appeared in *Modern Haiku, The Heron's Nest, Frogpond, Acorn, Chrysanthemum, Hedgerow, Haibun Today,* among others. Salil is the Asia-region winner of the Commonwealth Short Story Competition, 2008, and he won the Unisun/British Council Short Story Award in 2009. He also won the Wordweavers Poetry Contest in 2015. He brought out *Shabduli,* the first audio book in Konkani for visually impaired people in 2015. His work titled *Beautiful Women* documents the life of sex workers rehabilitated at a commercial laundry set up by ARZ, an NGO that works in the field of commercial sexual abuse in Goa. His debut poetry collection titled, *In The Sanctuary Of A Poem,* was released at the Goa Arts and Literature Festival in December 2017.

Kiran

Salil Chaturvedi

1.

from this
great
height I
jettison
(lavender-smelling Kiran, are you listening?)
my seed into the
night of Mumbai towards the
ovum of earth
passionately hoping that my
quintessence will mingle and
release a
species from extinction, if my love for the earth
has been true.

2.

Now they've built
a bridge, Kiran
which looks like your *asana*
over the Mapusa river
so that it's possible to traverse
it quickly (and quietly)
regardless of the time
and of the half-hourly
ferry and also without
the incendiary sips of feni
and the usual verbiage
at the water's edge —
in short, now one can cross
the river
without experiencing it.

3.

You say you don't remember
(you have absolutely no inkling?)
But I remember that lazy afternoon
when I applied the sun-tan lotion on your
back on Bogmalo beach. You said,
'my body is your canvas.'
I am devastated that
the memory exists
only in my brain.
Frenetically I've researched the matter and
gathered all the facts. It's amazing that all our
happiness (and all our opposite sorrows) reside
as invisible proteins attached to the end
of synapses. A jaded memory is simply
a contusion, an amino acid, enzyme
or exhausted reagent knocked out
sacrificing a precious illusion, my
lovely love protein, Kiran!

4.

At the lakeside,
by myself,
in a rare comma of existence
I discovered the great silence
(that you often speak of!)
Right there, on the edge
of the lake, I understood what you mean
when 'feel gravity through my buttocks,' you say.
A goat nibbling on the
grass looked up at me and
how, I don't know,
but it communicated
just how good the grass was.
Keenly I observed the silent syntax
of the Universe: the lingo of thrusts
and pinches, strokes and squeezes,
rubs and nibbles, these morphemes of the cosmos,
now you don't have to speak of them —
One wink will do.

5.

I much prefer this new clock, Kiran!
This keeper of time has no tics
(or heavy tocs)
Its hands run smoothly
in a serene circular glide
from moment to moment
not like the staccato and unreal nudges
of the previous clock.
Or do you think that nature keeps
time like that?
Perhaps our births and deaths
are a tic and a toc?

6.

Do you think they curse us?
(bi-petalled, single-stamened Kiran)
Even as they rise up
from their mutilated bodies,
these virgin souls of young
girls and boys
hacked by metal splinters
in their homes in Gaza
(and Burundi, Kashmir, Serbia, Syria ...).
Jealous are they of our
kamasutra nocturnes?
Let us knit our bodies on less
murderful nights.

7.

Blizzards, storm systems and cold-wave fronts were predicted
by the weather anchor last night, Kiran.
Extreme weather she presented —
ferocious winds over mountains like thrust boobs,
gusty winds and gales over powerful shimmering thighs,
warnings of hurricanes with perfect white teeth,
impending floods from melting ice over a taut black tummy,
jarring avalanches cascading down perfectly formed hips,
and an 18 karat gold chain dangling over delicately rounded
offshore winds,
lashing at scrumptious lips. The weather's been
maniacal and sexy.

8.

All sorts of criminals,
bad types,
crazies,
deviants, delinquents and
evil doers, when they
farm, the earth still offers them
germinating seeds that are
healthy and robust, even
illuminant — I'm so bewildered by the soil's
jurisprudence.

9.

As I sit in the hollow of this brook
deep in the Mollem forest
my bulging stomach facing upstream,
the cool water enters my navel
carrying a few tadpoles,
slim brown fish,
fragments of floating moss,
a red leaf,
the song of a Malabar thrush,
a monkey's shriek and
a flower of a Kumbiyo tree.
The water swirls around the depression in my back
between my fractured T10 and T12 vertebrae
and makes its way downhill,
already warned by the archives of my body
of what awaits it in the flat inventive plains.

10.

Conversations have become lethal, Kiran.
Our friendly verbiage
is eating the earth. A portion of a virgin Sahyadri forest loses
its hymen every time we pick up the cell phone
to incubate our love, dear
(that's two rose bushes,
a ladybug and a caterpillar you're holding to your ear).

11.

From this third floor flat in Dona Paula,
I see an egret fly over a clump of coconut trees,
a small waterhole in a green field,
and two moorhens building a nest around it.
And far away, on the Mandovi,
what look like incessant water ants —
the barges that work day and night,
carrying a bit of red Goa
heap by heap,
out to the waiting ships.
I can also see a crow riding out on a barge.
Perhaps they've taken his piece of earth this time.

12.

Is it possible Kiran
to love
just one of your smiles,
or to pour one's heart into
just one strand of your hair. To keenly adore
just one shoulder blade.
When it rains, is it possible to love just one ripple
even as it spreads out, magnifying
the circle of affection?
Is love to be niggardly and confined
to just one tree, one limb, one cloud,
one bird, one river, one sunrise,
one butterfly, one woman?

Mrinalini Harchandrai spent her childhood summers at her maternal grandmother's house in Goa, where she sped her cycle around corners, re-re-read comics and bounced around in Goa's warm ocean waves sans all the half-baked tourists. She is a writer, mostly based in Mumbai, and is the author of *A Bombay in My Beat* (Bombaykala Books, 2017), a collection of poetry that explores the soundtrack of the city, personal cadences and jazz poetry. She won first prize in *The Barre* (2017) and was longlisted for the Commonwealth Short Story Prize 2018. Her poems have also appeared in several literary journals. She is editor, co-publisher and chief pencil sharpener at Bombaykala Books.

Kitchen Drawer Guests

Mrinalini Harchandrai

They step out
when you sleep
or you've left the house

we gauge their size
from whorls in flour
or ant lines to fallen honey
they sleep with forks
dance with serving spoons
and fly on knife-like brooms
casting their spells
with spilled cashew apples
and jackfruit pits

sometimes you might see
their cat shine eyes
in passing car lights
sweeping the azulejos
or when the wind
takes the blame
for a fallen bowl
earthen, returned to source
before they flutter
leaving only the sugar dust
of wing gauze.

Ghosts

Mrinalini Harchandrai

There is a highway
of skulls, 'real India'
revved in
cracking open red
earth and lining Goa
with its asphalt ways.

A breeze undertows
the stench of a hill
that lies belly-up
the municipality
takes a siesta
while the insensate spin
green gold into trash
whales in whom echo
the detritus of reckless
sharks who stick decay
like flags here.

With the coin
of shrugging shoulders
the ministers point
to branchless trees, widening
the road of declassification
and axe coconut palm
vigilantes of luminous pastures
before they fall
on pirate skulls.

In the surf
plastic ghostfish
scooter silently
around our ankles
nearly grazing the sting
of lurking beer bottles.

The morning bread
cycles in with floury
habit in blue baskets
and drops on the headlines
while at the beach
rigor mortis sets in
the latest victim — violation
is always violent —
she came to sniff
a sunset haunt
and keeps becoming a crime
statistic that breaks
the heart of old-timers
living phantoms
who knew *fidalgo* days
of unlocked *portas*
and town dances.

The *communidade* well
ran dry and panchayats bid adieu
the first hippies, who now seek
to escape the grid
on the sands
of other oceans, while curry
rice is served in the shadows
lengthening by tetrapak counters.

Rochelle Potkar (see bio on page 74)

Confluence

ROCHELLE POTKAR

Waters when they evaporate, meet ...
at a global conference, to speak of fish dropouts,
obscura of clouds, near-deaths, hydrological dynamics,
monocultures and metals:
nickel, lead, chromium at their beds.

The bend is notional: water for coffee, cane,
banana, paddy,
mills, distilleries,
fertilizer plants.

The Aral sea was water for cotton
in Uzbekistan:
one shirt drinking 2,000 litres,
now more saline than the Dead Sea —
palm-sized, a fossil-tiger's footprint,

plains of salt, toxic dust storms,
fishing towns, now ship-graveyards.
people, sick; dumps of pathogenic weapons
making the summers hotter, winters colder,
the Aral Sea is the Aralkum desert.

And if seas made maps,
rivers, homes
men, borders.

The Cauvery too is uprising
one of the longest-running rivers
over her water share to ripple greens
for Karnataka and Tamil Nadu,
when her sand beds expand for mining
flowing from Brahmagiri
on her way to the Bay of Bengal,
she worries if those warring over her understand

that a river is a person,

like Whanganui of New Zealand
— ancestor of 140 years
that got legal status
through the longest-running litigation
by the Māori people

because mountains too
are equal to men.

Marinella Proença resides in Calangute, Goa, the village which inspired her first book of poetry *Heart Beat: Poems Awakening Goan Memories,* (Goa, 2008). It was released by the acclaimed artist, Mario Miranda, who also provided illustrations for the book. In 2008, Marinella was invited to release the book by the Goan Association in Canada, at the Global Goan Convention. The book has had a successful run, and it has been catalogued by 11 American Universities including Yale and Cornell, and it also sits on the shelves of The Library of Congress, Washington D.C..

Basanti Has Arrived ... Hallelujah!

MARINELLA PROENÇA

The cogu echoes its koyal song
glibly — pitching its scores along
spring's tapestry: of birthing pods
green arrows pinned to nudist fronds
And so I look for seasons' signs
Of new beginnings, evolving climes
that cheat ol' winter's wrinkled mind
with virtual treats: of mutiny.

Bumble-bee in black yet blue
locks musket-drawn on shoe-flower tube
Pinks and reds and yellows anew
marching forth through pin-hole view
Lepidop wings flit-tango along
Unrepentant — for their closet anon
But for them, journey's end begins upon
an orgasm: of colourful blasphemy.

The time it is — that time of year
When tonal tweets tune through the ear
Sweet altos, supes, even crow-pheasant gongs
entice their way through aural drums
And side by side hear cymbals crash
And dholls they roll — to gulal splash
When the cry of anointed Holi lads

spills over — to sensual cacophony.

Soon …
Our lamp is lit and doom dispersed
When wick ignites with impatient thirst
And clouds of darkness — draped in Light
And Holy-*agua* flings sin out of sight
Of Alpha … Omega — we rave in song
Be-el'zebul — sent packing along …

We're born again to a splendorous dawn
As each atom explodes — in synchrony.

LETTERS

Selma Carvalho (see bio on page 12)

The Letters of C. E. U. Bremner: Same Old Tired Prejudices

SELMA CARVALHO

Pacing his office, badly served by his predecessor and left in a 'chaotic condition,' Lieutenant-Colonel Bremner knew nothing good would come of his posting to Goa. Outside lay a land shorn of adventure, a land whose weather he found to be 'unbearably sultry,' whose Southern European colonisers spent their time in 'cheery inebriation,' militarily emasculated, administratively inefficient and civilisationally inferior to the Northern European nation of Britain.

He wore his bigotries like a tightly-knit vest and exercised them frequently in the course of his duties. He epitomised the last of his tribe, the diehard loyalist, who believed firmly in the moral rectitude of the Empire, and as the newly appointed Majesty's Consul for the Portuguese Possession in India, he shouldered bravely the white man's burden of keeping order in the world. It was November 1940, and Bremner was 49 years old.

Bremner: 'Sound Frontier Officer'

Claude Edward Urquhart Bremner[5] was born on 30 August, 1891, the son of Henry John Bremner and Edith Charlotte Graham. His father had served as a colonel in India, where Bremner and his sister Morgan were born but then Edith had returned to England with her

---

5. Confidential Reports on Captain C.E.U. Bremner of the Indian Political Service, IOR/R/I/4/1007, British Library, King's Cross, UK.

two children.[6] It was customary to 'ship' wives back for the children's schooling. The family belonged to the St. Peter's Parish in Bedford, where Bremner spent his early years. Possibly, Bremner knew from a young age that he would follow in his father's footsteps. He attended Bedford Grammar, a school inclined to preparing young men for the army. There he showed an aptitude for languages winning a prize in French. He qualified for Woolwich (Royal Military Academy) but opted instead to go to Sandhurst (Royal Military College) from whose ranks were drawn the bulk of the Indian Staff Corps. Here, he further honed his language skills becoming conversant in Urdu, Pashto, and Punjabi. Shortly after, in 1911, aged just twenty, he was commissioned into the army and arrived at Quetta.

Quetta spread before him, an inhospitable garrison town on the northwest frontier of British Baluchistan (administered by British India). It was a common enough destination for new recruits who continued their training there. These men, barely into adulthood, were ill-prepared for a life on the frontier. Most called it their 'term of exile' and endured its austerity in anticipation of a promising career ahead. Bremner appeared to be a 'cheery, energetic, hardworking and very companionable' recruit but his general ability was noted as 'upto the average.' By 1916,[7] he was already planning on joining the Foreign and Political Department of the Government of India, an appointment which finally came in 1919, as assistant political agent to Sibi.[8] There, Bremner carried out his duties as an 'earnest-minded,' if somewhat 'solemn' chap. More postings followed, including Panjgur and Waziristan. Initially at least, Bremner made a 'sound frontier officer' showing 'the greatest sympathy for and interest in Indians of all sorts.'

---

6. Edith Bremner is recorded as living with her two children at Bedfordshire on the 1901 Census records. Her husband is not listed.

7. During World War I, Bremner served in East Africa, and whilst stationed there, R.A. Lyall wrote a letter of recommendation for him to join the Foreign and Political Department of the Government of India.

8. The role of a political agent was to be the British representative in the region offering aid and advice to local chiefs.

Almost a century earlier, the explorer Richard Burton had
arrived at the 'glaring waste' of the northwest, as a young army
recruit for the East India Company, to be 'shot at sixpence a day.'
Like Bremner, Burton was adept at languages and used them to
cultivate relationships with local tribesmen. But there the similarity
ended. Burton developed a certain respect for the tribals who
he believed would rather declare, 'I am a Beloch and I will die
first,' than surrender in battle. To a man like Burton, raised on a
tutelage of fencing and wrestling, physical force was the epitome
of masculinity. Burton had embraced the volatile nature of the
subcontinent and earned himself the nickname 'white nigger.'[9]
Bremner, however, was not quite as hardy. Frequent tribal uprisings
on the frontier had left Bremner considerably 'nervy.' It was agreed
that he had 'been too much in out of the way places,' and that he
was to be transferred to 'where he can see more of his fellow men.'

Bremner: 'An Embittered Officer'

An interlude away from India came, in 1932, with a posting as
political agent to Muscat. Although the Arabian Gulf did not come
under the formal fold of Empire, the British nonetheless maintained
a strong influence in the region with appointed political agents who
reported to a political resident.

The Gulf Arabs were very different to the tribesmen Bremner
had encountered on the northwest border. In Muscat, the role
of political agent called for the ability to resolve issues using a
diplomatic nudge. Bremner worked conscientiously but the substance
of the man had altered, leading Political Resident Trenchard C.
Fowle (1932–1939) to think of him as 'an embittered officer.'

Given to writing long, rambling letters, it was reportage that
Bremner perfected rather than tackling problems head-on. Fowle
thought him a poor judge of character, impulsive, unable to size

---

9. The word 'nigger' has been retained in quotes only to reflect the terminology of
the times.

up situations and given to exaggeration. Bremner's utter failure in Muscat could not have been more complete than when Fowle wrote, 'For as long as I am Resident, I would prefer he did not return.'[10]

Excuses though were readily forthcoming — his health, the weather, his, at times good work — to mitigate Bremner's 'unbalanced' behaviour. Bremner was shielded from much of the discussions surrounding him. A dismissal was brushed aside in favour of a reshuffle.

In 1936, Bremner returned to India as political agent for the Sadar district. His short stay there did not end well. He complained bitterly about the primitive living conditions. He spent money from the Agency to buy himself dhurries, mattresses and curtains. A review of his work elicited even less enthusiasm than his indulgent expenditure. His immediate officer noted 'a tendency to express immoderate views on insufficient data or even no data at all.' The question of a transfer arose yet again. Now married to the twenty-three year-old Anne Geraldine Christian, who accompanied him to India, Bremner returned, in 1937, to Quetta. This posting too, proved to be a stopgap arrangement. Although competent, he was 'too easily prejudiced against individuals by gossip retailed to him.' His readiness to listen to gossip obscured his judgement. His shortcomings were thought to be not of a 'remedial' nature. A 'change of environment' was recommended.

Bremner Arrives in Goa: 'A Fascist State'
It was under this cloud of ignominy that Bremner arrived at Mormugao on 19 November, 1940. With him was his wife Anne. Their two young children, a nanny, three servants and two dogs were left behind in Belgaum where they'd taken up a bungalow with three acres of surrounding land. In Quetta, they had had an assistant Goan cook but it's not clear whether he accompanied them to Goa.

---

10. Bremner often took long leave on account of his health.

They drove from Belgaum to Goa. To Anne, the villages 'looked dilapidated … small, smoky huts between coconut palms and banyan trees.' Thin pariah dogs barked at them, men wore just loincloth and women, 'grubby cotton saris'; children ran around naked. Already, Bremner and Anne were disillusioned with what appeared to be the backwaters of the Indian subcontinent. The hinterland might have been dotted with ramshackle huts but they would not have been any different to thatched dwellings found in India. In actual fact, the nature of the *mundkar-bhatkar* (labour-landlord) relationship spared Goans the sort of land dispossession, homelessness and abject poverty evident in contemporaneous India.

Bremner, perhaps, believed he was being appointed to a position of strategic importance. Before the war, the resident engineer of the Madras and Southern Mahratta Railway at Mormugao had acted as the British vice-consul. These were generally honorary positions without a salary and their scope was limited to commercial and local interests. The British consul-general at French Pondicherry, Reginald C. F. Schomberg was overall responsible for Goa.[11] Schomberg's alarmist view of Goa as a receptacle of German propaganda and a 'fascist state' whose 'officials and leading citizens profess, admire and defend fascist principles'[12] had hastened the appointment of a full-time consul-general dedicated entirely to the affairs of the Portuguese territory. In reality the only thing that Goa experienced was the occasional drone of a far off plane, as Bremner was about to find out.

Bremner and Burton: 'Misleading and often inaccurate'

In 1847, explorer Richard Burton had arrived in Goa, a visit which prompted the scathing travelogue *Goa and the Blue Mountains* (1851). It is entirely possible that Bremner had read this book and was influenced by it; Burton, in turn, had no doubt been influenced

---

11. French India: British Consul-General at Pondicherry, IOR/L/MIL/14/72313, British Library, King's Cross, London.

12. Attitude of Portuguese India, FO371/26837, 1940-41, National Archives, Kew.

by the common banter in British cantonments about biracial and Christianised Asians being weak and effeminate. Bremner embraced Burton's untruths wholeheartedly throughout his stay in Goa.

To begin with, the Bremners were put up in Vasco at the Palácio Grande Hotel,[13] a 'grey stoned walled building' facing the sea, 'directly over the docks and the railway.' On one of the first days, they had been woken up at five in the morning by a local band playing 'Colonel Bogey.'

There was a tiny community of British residents in and around Vasco: The railway engineer and former vice-consul, a little man who was never able to make up his mind, and his wife, a large woman with a commanding voice; the harbour master responsible for the shipping that came into the harbour, and his wife; an Anglo-Indian man working for the railway who also helped out with war-time reporting, and his wife who loved gardening; captain of the dredger responsible for clearing silt from the harbour, and prone to drunken shouting at night; and representatives of the Burmah Shell Co and the Standard Vacuum Oil Co.[14]

The idea that Bremner would do well to be among 'more of his fellow men' was soon put to rest. His quickly drawn opinion of the British community was that they were insular, harbouring a 'superiority complex' and unfamiliar with 'the countryside beyond the roads to the railway station.'

Eventually a 'suitable house' was found for the Bremners in Panjim; the township a more appropriate location for the consulate. The house was on a hill, at the bottom of which was a 'Cathedral'[15] (Igreja de Nossa Senhora da Conceição). In front of the house was

---

13. The other hotel mentioned in Bremner's dispatches during this period is Spencer's Antigo Palace Hotel.

14. Standard Vacuum Oil Co was an American company and the representative might have been American.

15. Unpublished biography, Anne Bremner, *India during the British Raj,* MSS EUR F224 Goa pp 4, British Library, King's Cross, UK This description fits the Altinho, at the bottom of which is the Igreja de Nossa Senhora da Conceição.

a road across from a row of palm trees. Further up the hill were more houses, occupied by Germans. The Germans in question were Robert Koch,[16] a businessman later revealed to be a Nazi spy, and his wife Grethe. A short-term guest of the Koch's was Robert Hepp, a German engineer who had fled Bombay.[17] Shortly before Bremner's arrival, Goa had offered refuge to three German ships, the *Ehrenfels, Braunfels* and *Drachenfels*.[18] In July 1940, another Axis ship, the Italian SS *Anfora* also sought shelter at Goa.

Richard Burton's life was marked by contradiction and his prejudices were often at cross-purposes with his actions. (Despite his deep disdain for Goans, he hired Valentino Rodrigues[19] and Caetano Andrade, as personal servants to accompany him and Captain John Hanning Speke on their expedition to find the source of the Nile. These men became invaluable to Burton, and Burton acknowledged their contribution to the expedition.) Claude Bremner failed to

---

16. David Miller, *Special Operations, South-East Asia 1942–1945,* Pen and Sword, 2015, UK. Robert Koch arrived in Goa onboard the *Ehrenfels* in September 1939. Koch was later identified as the Nazi spy codenamed Trompeta. Koch and his wife Grethe took up a house in Panjim, from where Koch was rumoured to run espionage operations out of Goa. In December 1942, two British Special Operations agents, posing as businessmen, arrived in Goa, and after lunching with the Bremners, kidnapped the Kochs to across the border into British India. Although some suspect the Kochs might have been shot dead, it is more likely they were taken to Bombay to be interrogated.

17. British India had set up two civilian internment camps at Dehradun and Deoli, where a substantial number of Germans residing in India were incarcerated. Hepp was possibly fleeing internment.

18. Bremner reported frequently on the three German ships and the activities of the crew, who for the most part roamed around Goa freely, some even taking up local housing. As soon as he arrived, Bremner noted that a duplicate transmitter could still be on board one of the ships. He later suspected the ship captains of scheming to set up a transmitting set from rented accommodation at Anjuna. But he couldn't confirm this nor the suspicion that Koch was using a transmitter from his house in Panjim. A transmitter onboard the *Ehrenfels* was the most likely source of sailing information being transmitted to German U-boats in the vicinity. The refuging ships were destroyed in 1943 in a covert operation carried out by the Calcutta Light Horse auxiliary cavalry regiment.

19. Valentino Rodrigues proved to be extremely resourceful having learnt to use the chromometer and thermometer, and often taking charge of the porters. Andrade was fearless and once dived into crocodile infested waters to retrieve a gun. When Burton re-visited India in 1876, Rodrigues wrote to Burton hoping to see him.

show any such nuance in race relations. He regurgitated Burton's caricatured portrayals of Goans without investigation.

The consulate in Goa had attached to it two Indian intelligence officers but Bremner dismissed their reports as 'misleading and often inaccurate,' without proper knowledge of local conditions. Bremner's own summations of local conditions were equally suspect. The residents, he found to be in a state of 'mental depression' mired in recurring epidemics of typhoid, failing rice harvests, rising commodity prices and water shortages; the general despondency only ever lifted by frivolities such as Carnival, seen as an excuse to indulge in a 'complete drunken orgy,' during which time the elites put on fancy dress and raided each other's houses. The Easter that followed Lent was just an 'excuse for another orgy.'

Within a year of his arrival, Bremner had gleaned information that the Goan Catholic population, 'eagerly anticipated an early British occupation of Goa.' By December 1941, Bremner was writing: '*bazaars* and to lesser extent countryside are flooded with wildest rumours including that of imminent occupation of Goa by us [British]. This would generally speaking be welcomed by Goan Christians and the majority of the indigenous population groaning under taxation, grievances of top heavy maladministration, and injustice. Hindu trading community mostly pro-Congress and hence anti-British, would dread any such proposal.'

The idea that the Goan Catholic would have welcomed a British occupation and integration into British India, could have been little more than tea-table gossip. Was Bremner again falling into his old habit of relying on 'insufficient data or even no data at all'? Had Bremner, even peripherally, been engaged with the Goan Catholic community, he would have encountered a different perspective.

Nationalist Tristão de Bragança Cunha who founded the Comissão do Congresso de Goa (later as National Congress Goa affiliated to the Indian National Congress), decried the creation of a Lusitanised identity among the Goan Catholic, distinct and severed from the rest of the Indian subcontinent. In his 1944 booklet, *Denationalisation of Goans,* Cunha rued that, 'In the whole of India, no people is so denationalized as Goans. A complete lack of national consciousness … render the Goan and particularly the Goan Christian a stranger in his own land.' Later, Cunha became the chief publicist for the liberation movement through his paper *Free Goa,* published initially from Belgaum and then Fort, Bombay, from where, in exile, he continued to rail against the apathy of the Goan Catholic. Telo de Mascarenhas,[20] also a nationalist and no less a proponent of Goa's merger with India, nonetheless in 1953, ran an editorial in his paper *Ressurge Goa,* which articulated, this aspiration amongst Goans to be, in some manner or other, separate from Greater India. It read: 'The Prime Minister of India, Mr Nehru, has more than once expressed that Goa, in view of its culture, language and custom should after its integration, be an autonomous unit inside India. The Indian National Congress, in a resolution passed at Jaipur in 1949, has also guaranteed Goa such status. It is up to the National Congress Goa, if it is desirous of the support and cooperation of Goans, to back the declaration of the Prime Minister …'

Quite apart from a distinct identity, Goans carried within them a sense of exceptionalism, in part cultivated by their status as equal citizens. While, the Indian was a subject of the British empire, Pombaline reforms had ensured the Goan Catholic of equal status with the Metropolitan Portuguese, and later the Constitution of the First Portuguese Republic 1911, further fashioned a sense of nationhood by granting them citizenship.[21] During this period, substantial numbers from Goa migrated to British India and British East Africa in search of employment, but the aspiration was always to build a house and retire to a *sossegado* life in Goa. Richard Burton, a century before Bremner's arrival, had made this precise observation:

---

20. Further reading: Phd. dissertation of Lucas Mestrinelli, On the Eve of the End: Visions on the Future of Goa 2017, University of Campinas, São Paulo, Brazil.

21. Colonial Act 1930 rescinded many of these rights.

'Although poverty sends forth thousands of black Portuguese to earn money in foreign lands, they prefer the smallest competence at home, where equality allows them to indulge in a favourite independence of manner utterly at variance with our Anglo-Indian notions concerning the proper demeanour of a native towards a European.'

Once abroad, Goans invariably, gathered in communities alienated from Indians. They set up associations and clubs which nurtured this sense of separateness. The presidents of these associations were antagonistic towards any freedom movement which aligned with India. Instead, particularly in East Africa, they allied with Portugal's consular attachés.

Nor was life in Goa as dire as Bremner painted it to be. The chief township of Panjim was a mannered town with storeyed houses, and educational, literary and social institutions like the Liceu Nacional Central de Alfonso de Albuquerque, the Bibiloteca Nacional de Vasco da Gama (library), the Instituto Vasco da Gama (literary and scientific society) and the Clube de Nova Goa.[22] Elite Goan men were safely cushioned in jobs within the Portuguese administration or military service. Many lived off the revenue of their large estates or owned business ventures. A petite bourgeois class sustained itself as bakers and tailors. It is improbable that any substantial number of Goan Catholics would have wanted to put at risk the privileges Portuguese colonialism assured them of and anxiously awaited Goa's annexation by British India.

As his immediate reporting officer in Muscat had observed, Bremner was quick to form opinions and just as quick at reversing them. This is exactly what he did in Goa. By February 1942, Bremner was reporting on Goan pensioners from British East Africa, who, far from favouring Britain, were fermenting anti-British sentiments. 'Loyalty,' he wrote, 'is not a strong point in the make-up of any Goan, a point which is possibly unknown to those whose

---

22. Celsa Pinto, *Colonial Panjim: Its Governance, Its People,* Goa 1556, 2017.

association with this heterogeneous race is limited to superficial contact with cooks, clerks and bootlairs [butlers].'

Ironically, the disdain he felt for Goan clerks would have been misplaced in the context of East Africa, something he might have been unaware of, or chose to ignore. The Goan clerk formed the backbone of the British administration and without them, the experiment of empire itself might have collapsed. Hildegarde Beatrice Hinde, the anthropologist, wrote endearingly of Goans: these 'timid and sociable' men were willing to live 'under conditions that no Englishman of the clerk class would have tolerated.' They endured with fortitude, the loneliness of the remote *bomas,* were hardy enough to survive Africa's inhospitable terrain. Embedded in them was the sort of honesty which earned them a reputation as the keepers of all the safes in Kenya.

Bremner seemed determined to confirm every trope as truth; his penchant for assumption bordering on the absurd. When faced with a possible water shortage, Bremner thought the hardship would not be too great to bear, 'as most Portuguese only bathe sparingly at long intervals and Goans apparently never.' Always the loyal imperialist bringing civilisation to the world, Burton too had described the 'Black Christian Goans' as 'dirtier than Pariahs, and abound[ing] in cutaneous diseases.' While disease and dirt were common a century earlier, by the 1940s Goan families ritually heated, every evening, a large copper pot of water for bathing. Advances in hygiene were some of the more transformative changes experienced in 20th century Goa.

But the native as a carrier of disease lived on in the colonial imagination. The fear of being polluted meant Europeans could, with moral legitimacy, enforce a *cordon sanitaire* racially segregating themselves from non-European populations. And town planning authorities ensured that the areas they came to occupy were more salubrious, more fertile or more commercially viable than those allocated to local populations.

There were other popular myths for Bremner to peddle.

Convinced of the debased nature of Goan Catholics, he wrote: 'The student element, mostly composed of half-breeds, have been heard vaunting what they will do if the British attempt to seize Goa but much of the wind in their heads is likely to exude from other portions of their anatomy if and when that event occurs. They are the vain, but vapid result of tropical conditions on the dregs of human society.' Burton too had spilled scorn on the Goan 'half-breed' as being 'a strange mélange of European and Asiatic peculiarities, of antiquated civilisation and modern barbarism.'

The misconception, in part, encouraged by Goan Catholics, that they were largely mestiço prevailed through the 19th century and well into the 20th. In actual fact, a tiny portion of the population were biracial. What both, Burton and Bremner, were undoubtedly mistaking for mixed-breeding was the efficacy of Portuguese enculturation.

Bremner's contempt for biracial Goans as 'the vain but vapid result of tropical conditions,' was the stock excuse for the waywardly behaviour of European colonials; the heat and dust of empire, which led men astray, to drink, violence and cohabiting with the local *bibi.* These liaisons were not officially recognised; their mixed-race offspring were the *kutcha-butcha*[23] of Indian society and 'neither fish nor fowl' of British society, placated with subordinate roles in the administration, particularly supervisory posts in the railway.[24]

But the case of the Goan mestiço was not entirely parallel to that of their Anglo-Indian counterparts. Although some were illegitimate, a biracial marriage among local elites was a way of securing further social and political clout. Mestiço Goans occupied a secure and prominent role in society, secondary to that of white Portuguese but influentially positioned above the indigenous elite.

Bremner was by no means going to confine his clichés to just

---

23. A derogatory term meaning half-baked bread and used for biracial Indians.

24. Biracial Anglo-Indian children if baptised into the Protestant faith would be assisted with public financial support. Later policy dictated that only biracial children of legitimate marriages could be assured of public assistance.

Goans. Goa, after all, was a port of call for other non-European races. In early 1942, the sloop *Gonçalves Zarco* convoying *João Belo,* diverted from enroute to East Timor, docked at Mormugao Harbour. The expeditionary force onboard, a complement of European and Africans, were housed in barracks around Mormugao.

The African soldiers, Bremner thought to be 'negroes of fine physique.' This seemingly casual comment positions the 'negro' as an object. The African body inscribed with stories of chattelship was often exhibited at 'human zoos' as objects of curiosity. Burton for instance, kept detailed notes about the African body, including at one point, the size of the penis. The African was to be measured in terms of productivity, as one would a workhorse.

'Memories of the depredations of African troops' Bremner wrote, 'have been quickly revived and several Hindu families have already hurriedly removed themselves to safer areas … those who fear for their own safety and the chastity of their wives at the hands of the Negroes.' The indigenous Goan population whether Hindu or Catholic, even today, are not averse to racism of their own. The African, the *khampri,* is a figure of feckless stupidity and unbridled sexual appetite in the popular imagination. It could well be that Goans were reacting to the arrival of African troops, reinforcing Bremner's stereotype of the African as sexually dissolute.

Bremner: 'A Lonely Man'

By February 1942, the departure of the only naturally speaking English gentleman, an American, left Bremner in the 'unenviable position of splendid isolation.' What could he amuse himself with amidst unwashed locals and inebriated colonials? Decorum and duty necessitated, that he establish a relationship with the Portuguese Governor-General José Ricardo Pereira Cabral, a man who Bremner described as looking more like a stockbroker than a soldier. Still, Cabral spoke 'tolerably good English' and some French, was 'most courteous,' and had an 'immense sense of humour hidden behind a somewhat sphinx-like face.' Cabral was 59 when he arrived in Goa in 1938, along with his wife, Sara Albuquerque, and some of his children. Previously, he'd served in the enviable post of Governor-General of Mozambique (1926–1936). The former cavalryman was no stranger to the British. He had fought alongside the British during World War I in East Africa, and had been appointed an honorary Commander of the Order of St. Michael and St. George. In 1940, he was made an honorary Knight of the Order of the British Empire. This meant, Cabral and Bremner had something in common: both had seen action in East Africa during the war.

The Bremners and Cabrals formed an outwardly amicable relationship. Sara, a 'not unattractive lady,' was considerably younger than her husband. According to Bremner's accounts, Sara found Goa a 'most depressing spot' and she yearned for the civilisational pleasures of Lourenço Marques. Anne Bremner found Portuguese etiquette to be anachronistic. 'At parties the women sat around the room in order of rank. The Governor's wife at the head … No unmarried woman could sit beside a married woman. The girls at the end had to sit in order of their father's status.' The men stood around the bar talking to each other.

Goa remained insulated from the raging war[25] and nothing, it seemed, inhibited the general merriment in the capital township. The Bremners entertained frequently; an Easter Ball and two cocktail-dansants were held soon after their arrival. 'The worse that the news was from the war zone the bigger and better parties' were held. On one occasion, the Governor-General overcame his usual reticence and asked Anne to dance. Much socialising took place at a bar in Miramar. The Portuguese women arrived dressed in fine clothes, hats, jewellery and high-heels, and they whiled away their time gossiping and playing Mahjong.

---

25. Although Goa did not experience fatalities during World War II as a result of direct engagement, it endured a great loss of Goan seamen working onboard British ships.

Bremner promoted himself as a catalyst for change in Anglo-Portuguese relations. Even the manager of the Burmah Shell Company, he alleged, had expressed 'amazement at the completely changed attitude of Portuguese officialdom and society, who formerly were so very anti-British.' His actual relationship with the Portuguese in Goa was of little diplomatic consequence.[26] Schomberg who visited Bremner had an inkling his influence was of a superficial nature, fearing it would disappear if Bremner 'were to make any approach on a serious issue.' Schomberg knew Bremner had already proved inadequate. The British had requested the Portuguese to maintain a blackout in Goa, in keeping with war-time practices observed on the Indian subcontinent. As one Government of India official put it, 'While we should not be greatly concerned if Goa is bombed we should prefer it not to serve as a landmark to hostile aircraft.' But Cabral was reluctant to bow down to British pressure, instead, deferring the matter to Lisbon. Bremner was unable to lend weight to the negotiations.

Bremner was a 'lonely man' and had confided in Schomberg a desire to be posted to Nepal. O. K. Caroe,[27] of the External Affairs Department in Simla, was having none of it, pegging Bremner as a 'difficult [person] to deal with wherever he is.' Caroe thought little of Bremner's abilities, writing in 1942: 'He is inclined to dramatise himself and his work, and his reports and advice are not always distinguished for a wise perspective. These aspects are a part of his nature, and are, I fear incurable.'[28] In 1943, M.O.A. Baig took over from Bremner as the British consul-general for Goa.

---

26. During Bremner's time in Goa, he met Archbishop D. José da Costa Nunes who he described as a 'Portuguese gentleman of culture and great personal charm.'

27. Secretary to the Government of India in the External Affairs Department, Simla.

28. There is no archival trace of Bremner's career after Goa. It is possible he returned to England. Bremner died on 25 April 1965.

LITERARY ESSAYS

Paul Melo e Castro (see bio on page 92)

Portuguese Language Goan Literature: Whence, Whither and Wherefore?

PAUL MELO E CASTRO

In *India: A Million Mutinies Now,* a book as much lauded for its style as censured for its polemics, V. S. Naipaul writes:

> "[t]he Portuguese had created in Goa something of a New-World emptiness, like the Spaniards in Mexico. They had created in India something not of India, a simplicity, something where the Indian past had been abolished. And after 450 years all they had left behind in this emptiness and simplicity was their religion, their language (without a literature), their names, a Latin-like colonial population, and this cult, from their cathedral, of the Image of the Infant Jesus." (1990, p.142)

Even the most cursory glance at the sizeable body of literature in Portuguese from Goa demonstrates the many ways in which this assertion, redolent of stereotypes about Goa peddled both in India and Europe, is simply erroneous. Rather than any emptiness, Goa as pictured in its Portuguese-language archive, presents a highly complex mix of autochthonous and Portuguese elements, pre-Gama inheritances and British influences, and a population separated yet also conjoined by differences of caste, class and religion only characterisable as simple from an exterior position of ignorance or bias.

In no way was the Indian past abolished, though perhaps to call it Indian in a national, as opposed to ethnic or civilisational sense might be anachronistic. Instead Goa was and is a product of manifold influences on the ground from both East and West and a global history connected to the seaways of the Indian Ocean and beyond. As regards the other characteristics Naipaul seized upon: Portuguese-derived names and the Catholicism they indicate are, it is true, commonplace in Goa today though among a steadily decreasing percentage of its inhabitants.

The Portuguese language, he believed to be general, plays a relatively small role in the life of the territory at present, though the vast yet fragile written archive in that tongue is a rich resource that could be better known and utilised. To disclose some of it to an English-speaking audience is an objective of my own work. Here — as a small rejoinder to Naipaul's airy denial of its existence and from my admittedly limited position as a British academic specialising in Portuguese and comparative literature — I shall reflect on the sources of Portuguese-language writing in Goa, the fate of this body of writing today, and the various uses to which it — alongside the other languages of Goan literature Naipaul entirely omits to mention — could be put to service in wider engagements with Goa, India and the Portuguese-speaking world.

The status of the Portuguese language speaks volumes about the break in Goan history in 1961. If Portuguese is now a distant third language in local schools and used only in a scattering of homes, such a reduced role is a post-colonial development. By the mid-19th century, according to Sandra Lobo, a significant portion of Goan Catholics to all intents and purposes spoke Portuguese as a mother tongue. Indeed some, such as Elgar Noronha, see its use as having penetrated more deeply into society than English in neighbouring territories during the Raj, an idea testified by its influence on the Konkani of Catholics whose families would never have been functionally Lusophone. Nevertheless, Portuguese never attained what Dilip Loundó calls a 'self-reproducing linguistic structure.' Quickly disestablished after 1961, with the officialization of Konkani in the Devnagari script in 1987, and the expansion in the use of India's associate official language, English, Portuguese was extirpated rapidly from public discourse.

This discontinuation of Portuguese has meant that Goan writing in that tongue has been little researched either in Goa, where few people have the language skills or inclination to confront the task, or in the Lusophone world, where the overriding focus has been the countries and territories that retained Portuguese as an official language.

Today the situation appears to non-Portuguese speakers that Goan writing in Portuguese is limited to 'a few turgid, unwieldy novels and some vacuous quasi-mythological poetry' (Shetty, 1998, p.xvii). Given the hearsay upon which such an opinion must necessarily be based, there is a need to map out accurately and honestly the extent and import of Goan writing in Portuguese via means accessible to a modern Goan/Indian readership. One avenue is the translation of primary texts. Another way is the mobilisation Portuguese-language writing to think through the cultural history and social development of Goa and Portuguese colonialism within the dynamics of the Indian subcontinent. And to demonstrate its importance as a source of material with which to reflect on the roots of the present day.

Yet scholars and readers in/of India are not the only readership that Goan writing in Portuguese might interest. This archive, in part, because of its repertoire of styles, influences and references, provides immediate bridges with the Lusophone world, a considerable cultural resource for a small territory that is peripheral to the teeming Indian nation and to which, like all small entities, multilateral connections are vital. For scholars of postcolonial Portuguese-language writing, the Goan archive presents significant particularities, many of which can help denaturalise, reframe or extend debates in the field.

As Portuguese did not survive Goa's decolonisation as a hegemonic language, it did not become, as in Africa, a unifying tongue of postcolonial nation building. Instead it was left a minority concern, a sort of dwindling *bhasha* in families where it had been adopted as an intimate medium of communication or for those whose educational and working life had been conducted exclusively in Portuguese until that point. Some of the peculiarity of post-1961 Goan literature can be attributed to this situation. This status as an outlying and sui generis example of what Abdul Jan Mohammed and David Lloyd term a minority discourse (1990) warns against the generalisations occasioned by the language's status elsewhere.

Contrary to Lusophone Africa, yet similarly to Portugal's other Asian enclaves — though the difference between Goa and Macau and Timor-Leste are perhaps greater than their likeness — Goa's decolonisation did not result in the immediate constitution of a new nation state. Rather Goa was absorbed into greater India, which meant that the traditions and institutions deriving from its colonial past, such as language, were largely overlaid and displaced by those of British India.

One hegemonic construction gave way to another divergent vision of history and society, though it would be an oversimplification to conceptualise this shift as a rack focus between *Goa Dourada,* or Goa as an Europeanised outpost of Portugal, and *Goa Indica,* a pimple from which the colonial pus, to extend a metaphorical description of the Estado da Índia attributed to Jawaharlal Nehru, had finally been squeezed, leaving its fundamentally Indian culture to blend unblemished back into the face of Mother India. According to Rosa Maria Perez, these two discourses, first binarised in academic discourse by Caroline Ifeka, actually co-exist in bespoke ways among the various stakeholders in Goa's identity. Goan literature in all its languages, with the dialogism inherent to this form, becomes a privileged site for mapping out these fractious connections. If, as Rochelle Pinto has argued, Goa (like Portugal in the 19th and early 20th centuries) has had to measure itself by its deviation from the Imperial British Indian model, this disparity only grew with the engrossment of the former *Estado da Índia* to what Salazar cussedly referred to as the Indian Union. The body of Goan literature produced under colonialism forms a discontinuous cartography of Goan attitudes to colonial rule and the possibility of escaping its bounds, European intellectual currents and changing local traditions, from the late nineteenth century to the post-1961 period.

Though 1961 impelled a dramatic socio-linguistic shift in Goa, it should not be taken, however, that a familiarity with the English language and the institutions of India was previously absent. An irony of history is that as Portuguese citizens, Goans played a prominent role in the British Empire. Indeed, the English language was a prominent language of education in Goa at least by the end of the 19th century, as shown in the stories of José da Silva Coelho, the most prolific Goan fictionist of the 1920s. Albeit tacitly encouraged by an administration in need of migrant remittances, this internal prominence of English caused dismay amid senior Portuguese figures in the colony, such as the Portuguese Patriarch of the East Indies, Dom José da Costa Nunes, who, as Sandrine Bègue tells us, upon arriving in Goa in 1940, found himself resorting to English in order to address school children. An examination of the Goan scene as expressed in its literature brings home the postcolonial fact that no society can be reduced to a single position on colonialism, language, decolonization or hierarchy, whatever hegemonies are in operation. As the Portuguese geographer Orlando Ribeiro puts it, in a rather Orientalist simile, 'Like some Hindu gods, who have three faces and six arms, the truth about Goa is […] various and movable.' Goan literature, in both its successes and its *partis pris,* gives ample testament to this fact.

As such Goan writing in Portuguese, whether in the original or in translation, is of interest to readerships interested in Goan writing in any language and to a contemporary Lusitanist community whose centre of research is the Atlantic space where Portuguese is at its most dominant. For the latter, the sui generis colonisation and de-colonisation of Goa, not to mention its current status as the phantom limb of Lusophony, provides a literary space in which the key categories and terms of postcolonial theory — the ways in which, to reprise the words of Cristina Bastos, 'colonialism produced hierarchised states of being, staying, expressing feelings and thoughts, making political statements, defining identities, generating relationships' — can be compared, challenged and relativised. Again contrary to other Lusophone literary systems, which at most draw on other local languages as a differentiating resource, Portuguese-language writing in Goa sits alongside three other major bodies of writing in Konkani, Marathi and English. Even when, as here, the focus is on Portuguese-language writing, the ultimate approach to Goan writing must be comparative, albeit a comparativism challenging any traditional notion of the field as most properly juxtaposing national traditions.

Helena Carvalhão Buescu has understood lusophone *literatura-mundo* to form 'different observation points in Portuguese, according to the historical-symbolic, geographical and cultural dimensions that are illuminated.' For her this corpus should be 'understood as the simultaneous experience of the shared and the distinct: an archive of possible similarities but also of differences and infinite variations.' Here I add the simple point that including literary production from Goa (and other Asian spaces where Portuguese has been used) enhances the 'sphericity' of this experiential world and allows its intellectuals to view key issues in the round, even as Goa's multi-lingual, intra-imperial literary history provides a compelling reminder of the critical need to transcend linguistic blocs calqued on colonial world divisions.

Even as we reach, perhaps asymptotically, the end of Portuguese-language Goan literature as a living tradition — though unexpectedly, in recent years, works as interesting and varied as Ave Cleto Afonso's resourceful mini epic *O Vaticínio do Swârga* (2013) and Epitácio Pais's disabused novel of Indira Gandhi-era Goa *Preia-Mar* (2016) have materialised — many avenues of exploration remain open to critics of this writing. There persists a need to sift through the archive, to consider bodies of work that are little studied, often due to being unavailable in Portugal, such as the 1960s poetry of Laxmanrao Sardessai either composed originally in Portuguese or 'transcreated' from Konkani,[29] the *crónicas* of Walfrido Antão or Evágrio Jorge in the 1960s and 1970s, or the short fiction of Augusto do Rosário Rodrigues from the 1970s and 1980s, just to name writers that interest me personally. There is a vital need to build up a more complete understanding of the nineteenth and twentieth-century Portuguese-language print culture of Goa, which, undigitalised, remains under threat of disappearance. In this context we might consider, for instance, the analyses of Portuguese rule in this period provided, in and out of the Portuguese-language, by figures such as Luís de Menezes Bragança (1878–1938), the Konkani activist Waman Ragunath Shennoi Varde Valaulikar, popularly known as Shennoi Goembab (1877–1946), José Inácio Cândido de Loyola (1891–1973), and Tristão de Bragança Cunha (1891–1958). In all its languages, Goan writing offers vantage points from which to consider the nature of a certain strain of Portuguese colonialism and contributes to a fuller understanding of the anti and post-colonial ideas and attitudes developed against the practices and discourses of Portuguese imperialism.

If the majority of Goa's Portuguese-language writing is unknown to the territory today, similarly much in English remains to be translated into Portuguese, in whose cultural space the considerable

---

29. A collection of original poetry alongside its English translation, and a very useful introduction by D. A. Smith appeared entitled *Avante, Goeses, Avante: The Portuguese Poetry of Laxmanrao Sardessai*, Goa, 1556, 2017.

body of writing in English, Konkani and Marathi critically representing the colonial past is almost entirely unknown. Given the great expansion of postcolonial studies connected to the former Portuguese empire, we can ponder the reasons why Lambert Mascarenhas's *Sorrowing Lies my Land,* a firebrand anticolonial novel published in 1956, in Bombay, and written just as the first domino of Portuguese imperialism was toppled with the liberation of Nagar-Dadra-Haveli in 1954, still awaits a Portuguese version.

Yet the body of Goan writing most inaccessible and incompletely known in the West is that composed in the two principal *bhashas* — Indo-Aryan languages — of the territory. Just in terms of literary works that could illuminate analysis of Goan fiction in Portuguese we have Laxmanrao Sardessai's 1930s Marathi novella *Mandovi! Tum Attlis?* (Mandovi! Have You Dried up?), an early piece of anticolonial fiction concerning the Third Portuguese Empire; Bakibab Borkar's Marathi-language *Bhavin* (1950), which Manohar Malgonkar describes as 'a faithful portrayal of … the twilight years of Portuguese Goa; a story of lust and passion against the background of a clash of cultures, Hindu and Christian, and the love-hate relationship between the rulers and the ruled' (1982, p.183). Indeed, of the latter, author Malgonkar goes as far as to say that '[i]f Luís de Camões was the trumpeter of Goa's Portuguese conquest, Bakibab Borkar was the poet who floodlighted the end of Portuguese rule' (1982, p.183). Unfortunately non-Marathi speakers can only take Malgonkar's word on this; cultural circulation between Marathi and Portuguese is practically non-existent.

The blossoming of Konkani-language writing in the Nagari alphabet after 1961 featured many resonant works dealing with the colonial period. These included texts as varied as Sheela Kolambkar's renowned short story *Guerr,* which appeared in English in Peter Nazareth's *Pivoting on the Point of Return* and in Portuguese in Alberto de Noronha's *Onde o Moruoni Canta,* and the essayistic writings in Konkani that Laxmanrao Sardessai produced towards the end of his life. A fine example of this is 'The Goan Baker' that appears in Jerry Pinto's anthology *Reflected in Water*. The latter concerns a Catholic who sneaks in messages to political prisoners at Fort Aguada by means of his 'Westernised' bread. Relatively little of these Konkani works has been translated into English, however, and even less into Portuguese. Of Konkani works written in the Roman alphabet and using the various Catholic *Mundarte,* which differ significantly from the officialised version of Konkani, little systematic knowledge appears to have be available at all.

As even this tiny selection indicates, there exists in Marathi and Konkani(s) a sizeable archive relating to Portuguese colonialism inaccessible to scholars without the requisite language skills. As a thought experiment, we can reflect on how our understanding of Portuguese postcolonial literary studies might shift if such material were brought to bear on Western understanding of the Portuguese colonial world. Yet, equally, if inverted in polarity, we might wonder how contemporary debates on the limits and formation of Goan society, history and identity would be re-configured if current actors had unfettered access to the full archive of textual material from the past in Portuguese, both literary and extra-literary. These, it must be stressed, are Goan texts, made of Goan materials to Goans designs, like the woven palms of yesteryear — *mollam* in Konkani, *olas* in Goan Portuguese — used as protective awnings. If any full analysis of Portuguese-language literary works from Goa urges an engagement beyond the bounds of the Portuguese language, here it must be recognised that an equal and opposite movement is to be desired, even if any instantiation of this remains largely outside the purview of my own work. In this spirit, this short text represents an opening bid in what I hope will be a long and fruitful conversation.

Glenis M. Mendonça was born in the village of Porvorim, Goa. She spent her childhood in the nearby town of Mapusa and graduated from St. Xavier's College, Mapusa. She read English for her Masters Degree which she completed at Goa University, securing a gold medal. From 2001, she has held the title of Assistant Professor at the English Department of Carmel College Goa. In 2017, she successfully defended her thesis, *Konkani Fiction in English Translation: A Critical Study,* for her PhD. Besides bringing Konkani fiction to an English readership through translation works, she is passionate about music, and is a member of the troupe *Goenchim Kirnaam,* performing often at *mando* festivals. She lives in Panjim, Goa, with her husband and two children.

The Konkani Short Story: Amplifying Unheard Voices

GLENIS M. MENDONÇA

The short story is a favourite among Konkani readers due to its brevity, realistic setting, tension-filled well-knit plot and limited characters, familiar and inspiring. In this time-conscious world where lengthy fiction seems stretchy and listless, it is the short story which can be read over a single sitting. At times, there are sub-plots that may make the short story a bit longer. Hence in contemporary vernacular, the term *katha* or story, is used and not *laghu katha* or 'short story', as its length has become negotiable.

Konkani literature can boast of a treasure-chest of stories, handed down over generations in an oral tradition or a written form. However, most of them are available to the Konkani reader sans translation into English. Translation into English is available of select stories by specific noteworthy writers like Damodar Mauzo who has published three collections into English as books *(These Are My Children, Teresa's Man and other Stories and Mirage)* or Jayanti Naik *(The Salt of the Earth)*. The other stories are published in anthologies like *Ferry Crossing* and *The Harvest* (ed. Manohar Shetty) or noticed in stray books published by Katha, IMB — Goapuri, Sivasankari, Sahitya Akademi, *Goa Today* of the 1980s and '90s, and the *Navhind Times* — the *Panorama* of the '90s. Many lie in the translator's frozen PC folders, waiting for a good editor to approach them and suggest publication.

The modern Konkani story begins with Shennoi Goembab *(Vaman Varde Valaulikar),* the pioneer of the Konkani literary Renaissance. *Mhoji Ba Khoim Gueli* (Where has my Ba Gone?), his first story was published in the magazine *Novem Goem* and was later included in the collection of the stories entitled *Gomanto Upanishad* (Vol. I 1928). This poignant story presents the pathos of the six-year-old Babulo who has lost his mother and desperately seeks to eternally reunite with her through death. One can juxtapose the plight of Babulo with the Konkani society who were forcibly weaned from their native language by Portuguese colonisers and yearned for their *mai-bhas* (mother-tongue). This story thus becomes emblematic of the Konkani people and their predicament. It was translated by Rashmi Rathi and published in *Goapuri,* Oct–Dec 1999.

In another story, *Vassushennoili Popai* (The Papaya of Vasu Shenoy), the papaya plant speaks in first-person, and narrates its own woeful saga after a strong wind blows it down. On similar lines is *Babumamalo Ponnos* (Uncle Babu's Jackfruit) where a jackfruit tree pours out its agony after human beings heartlessly pluck its raw and ripe fruit. In both these narratives, there is a noticeable anthropomorphism, where non-human beings are given human qualities. The *ponnos* and *popai* tell their woeful tales reminiscent of the Goan people who felt heartlessly exploited and braved the storms of the colonial regime. Goembab's stories hold a mirror to Goan customs and traditions and draw sprightly pictures with a streak of humour. There is always an underlying message to behave with moderation, be tolerant and just. Exuding the flavour of nostalgia and rusticity, his stories re-create the village scene in our minds.

Among the camp of Konkani story writers, Chandrakant Keni holds a significant space. He has to his credit five collections of short stories: *Bhuim Chanfi, Dhortori Ozun Jietali, Ashaddh Panvlli, Olmi* and *Vhonkol Paunni.* Most of his stories abide by the maxim 'Show, don't tell.' Keni, a journalist by profession, says that his stories are like delicate drawings with no gaudy colours, suggesting much more than what they express. With a twist at the end, most of his stories like *Lucy, Vhonkol Paunni* and *Hippie Girl* are bold and effortlessly narrated. Keni has introduced innovations to the narrative of the Konkani short story. He uses monologue, diary entries and stories with a twist at the end which he calls the 'Kathika form.' Several of his stories are translated into English as also in other languages.

Damodar Mauzo bears a felicity as a storyteller in Konkani, who has managed to get most of his works translated into English, thanks to the efforts of translators like Vidya Pai, Sacheen P. Raiker, Augusto Pinto and Xavier Cotta. His translated short story collections include *These Are My Children* (2013), *Teresa's Man and other Short Stories from Goa* (2014) and *Mirage* (2015), the last one being a translation of longish stories (Deergh Katha) from *Rumadful* (1988). His writings display economy, precision, objectivity while displaying his experience and painstaking experimentation. Most of his characters are from lived experiences. As a curious listener, he claims to draw insights from clients who visit his grocery shop in South Goa. *Terezalo Ghov,* translated as Teresa's Man, portrays the jealousy of a house-husband over snide remarks made about his stylish wife's fashions. The inherent strain of patriarchy is obvious and the penchant of Mauzo to deal with Christian characters is noticeable. The predicament of poverty-stricken Christian farmers who are in a dilemma whether or not to sell their endearing cattle in order to make ends meet, is amplified in *Coinsanvalim Gorvam,* translated as 'Coinsanv's Cattle.' Stories like *Morn Iena Mhunn* and *Ani Hanv Portolom,* are suffused with an eco-sensitive verve. While the former makes a thirsty water-snake scramble for safety, to philosophise on life and the importance of nature preservation, the latter narrates the adventures of an elderly man who attempts to live sage-like in a forest, but seeing the birds returning to their nests, feels terribly homesick. Displaying a streak of Kafka or Camus, Mauzo's stories speak at times of existentialist ideas, but are still earthy and touch a chord of familiarity. The thread of Goan culture and ethos runs through his plots; the underlying messages are covert and subtle.

Pundalik Naik is one of the most prolific short story writer who pictures rural Goa in his writings. With a Konkani using racy, picturesque and vigorous words, his stories though regional, have a touch of universality about them. Naik is a versatile dramatist and novelist, but short stories come to him naturally and spontaneously. *Pixantar* (1977), *Mutthoi* (1977) and *Aardhuk* (1989) are his short story collections. The title story *Pixantar* revolves around the theme of unrequited love. Naik's stories like *Denth, Kasoi, Paraz* and *Voll* are arresting tales told in a language which is familiar and rustic-sounding. The Goan hinterland is explored; the aroma of paddy fields and the sight of coconut palms, fishermen at their nets and areca-groves watered by canals, form an integral part of his milieu. Himself a peasant, he is realistic in his portrayals and laces his narrative with sensuous poetry. *Kasai* translated as The Turtle by Augusto Pinto (*Goa Today*, Feb 1989) and Vidya Pai (*Ferry Crossing,* 1998), reveals the pitiable penury of fishermen who are compelled to flout tradition to make ends meet. The fisherman Vasu, despite knowing how sacred the turtle is to fishermen, finally sells it for a pittance to buy rice to feed his family. Naik's stories display heart wrenching scenes of traditions losing ground to the need for survival. While Mauzo finds the Christian life of South Goa as his fond subject, Naik delves deep into the rustic and agrarian hinterland of Goa.

In one of his published interviews, Mauzo has named the four stalwarts who gave the Konkani short story in the 1970s and '80s, its veracity. They include Mauzo (himself), Chandrakant Keni, Meena Kakodkar and Sheela Kolambkar. Among the several other Konkani short story writers (some who are translated into English) are Chandrakant Keni, Mahabaleshwar Sail, Meena Kakodkar, Sheela Kolambkar, Gajanan Jog, Vasant Bhagwant Sawant, Uday

Bhembre, Prakash Parienkar, Shashank Sitaram and Prasad Nilkanth Malkarnekar. These are but a few noteworthy names, though there are several more. Among the women story writers, the contributions made by Meena Kakodkar, Sheela Kolambkar, Jaimala Danait, Hema Naik and Jayanti Naik, are significant.

It was considered prestigious in the 1970s to be published in journals like *Jaag, Chittrangi* and *Kulaagar*. Most of the Konkani short stories appeared in such journals The authors then compiled their works (short stories) and knit them together in a host of publications. *Dhartari Aajun Jietali* (1964) by Chandrankant Keni is one of the earliest, followed by *Aashad Panvli* (1973), *Eklo Eksuro* (1973) and *Aalmi* (1975) — all by the same author. There were others like N. Shivdas's *Galsari* (1981), Olivinho Gomes' *Man Voddta Voddna* (1981), Gurudas Bambolkar's *Bhingar* (1977) and Ramkrishna Zuarkar's *Amcheo Khabro* (1981). All these were short story collections which added to the growth and thematic veracity of the Konkani short story in Devanagari script. However, these were male voices roaring in Konkani and very often in English translation. Sadly, the voices of the Konkani women short story writers went unnoticed to an English reader as they remained untranslated into English.

There is an interesting and vast treasure of short fiction written by women writers in Konkani. Sheela Naik Kolambkar has her short stories in collections like *Oli Saanz* (1973) and *Geurra* (2007). *Dongor Chavarla* (1976) and *Aami* (2011) are Meena Kakodkar's collections of stories. A mention has to be made of Jaimala Danayat's *Kavaso* (1978), *Saanz-Savli* (2014) and *Zopallo* (2016), besides, Hema Naik's *Durgavtaar* (2009) and Maya Karangate's Vishwa Konkani Sahitya Puraskar winning *Kapyalem* (2013). Stories from these collections written by women authors are voices from the margins, muffled by patriarchal traditions and need to be made audible to a global audience through wider translation.

Prakash Thali's translation of Sheela Kolambkar's, *Guerra,*

(Portuguese loanword for war) into English, published in the popular magazine *Femina* in 1974, may be considered as one of the earliest (known) translations of a Konkani short story. Post-translation, this story opened itself to wider research vistas, as much later it was translated into Portuguese by Alberto de Noronha. Hema Naik's title story *Durgaavtar* translated as The Resurrection, aims at subverting the patriarchal mould. Set in the mining belt of Goa, it recounts the audacious tale of Durgem, who suffering physical torture from her abusive, drunk husband, silently rejoices after murdering him and sleeps over the dead corpse which she buries under her dung-smeared floor. Thread with feminism of a rare kind displayed by rural women, Naik's narratives are engaging tales which amplify the subaltern voice of Konkan women. Tales from Hema Naik's *Durgaavtar* debunk the myth of the stereotypical self-sacrificing woman created by male writers.

Jaimala Danait's *Kavaso* (1978) is remarkable for using unique points-of-view as her narrative technique. *Paal* ('Lizard' as translated by Glenis M. Mendonça, *Joao Roque Literary Journal,* 2018) is narrated from the perspective of two lizards discussing the predicament of a household in mourning after the death of their elderly mother. The tragic end presents a wall as a symbol of division which separates not just a close-knit joint family but also the two inseparable lizards. *Kavllo-Kavlin* uses birds to voice the predicament of life in a complex world. Likewise, select stories from Jayanti Naik's *Athaang* (2002) have been translated into English as *The Salt of the Earth* by Augusto Pinto. These too hold a mirror to the traditions and ethos of rural folk who represent the subaltern voices of the *Bahujan* community, often smothered by powerful upper castes.

The journey of the Konkani short story has been one of extensive growth and innovation. More and more writers emerged, the themes in the stories were a myriad and the short story grew from a gurgling brook to a gushing stream where writers and publishers joined hands to come out with publications of short story collections. Though initially they were published in newspapers or were part of the fiction column of '90s' magazines, they gradually drew popularity and were republished in journals and books. However, only a few short stories caught the eye of translators and were translated into English and other foreign languages.

There is an urgent need to translate more Konkani short fiction into English. Stories by Konkani women writers are inaccessible to researchers and students without an English translation. They represent hidden voices which need to be also acknowledged as the zeitgeist of their times. These hitherto unheard narratives need to be read and critically studied by readers and researchers alike, so that the arena of Konkani literature grows richer with kaleidoscopic perspectives.

Jugneeta Sudan has lived in Goa for the past nine years — the longest in any one place since her birth in Udhampur, Jammu and Kashmir. With her peripatetic lifestyle, she feels she belongs nowhere but everywhere. This rootlessness has helped her imbibe Keats's principle of 'negative capability.' In her journey with literary criticism, she has focused on children's classic literature, Western classical texts, art history and poetry. In her writings she emphasises the importance of 'critic as an artist.' In *Navhind Times,* Goa her byline 'Booked and How' featured books and authors for five years, and presently she contributes articles on art and culture to *Daily O',* India Today Group. She has curated talks on contemporary art — *Raza Dialogue,* with Raza Foundation, Delhi and Museum of Goa, and an evening of poetry, art and music at the Goa pavilion — Serendipity Arts Festival, 2017. She heads PAG, the poetry appreciation group at Bookworm and has been recently shortlisted for the non-fiction award, 2018 by the *Joao Roque Literary Journal.* A lifelong seeker, she loves to travel and visit arty towns all over the world. She lives with her husband and son.

Camões in Goa — The Journey of an Epic

JUGNEETA SUDAN

Despite his far-reaching influences on European, American and South African writers, the great Renaissance poet Luís Vaz de Camões (1524–1580) remains one of the best-kept secrets outside of Portugal and its colonies. The title of his epic poem *Os Lusíadas,* literally means the descendants of Lusus, the mythical ancestor of the Portuguese, and the poem is a monument to the heroic deeds of Lusitanians. The courage and enterprise of Portuguese oceanic explorations, most notably Vasco da Gama's discovery of a sea route to India, is presented in a Homeric fashion and is the central theme in the epic. Around this, is portrayed in the ekphrastic tradition, the history and destiny of the Portuguese race.

Camões has been eulogized by many, including Italian poet, Torquato Tasso's sonnet 'Rime d'Encomio' — 'feared no man but Camões,' Blake's painted portrait of Camões and Wordsworth's literary veneration, 'Camões, he the accomplished and the good/ Gave to thy fame a more illustrious flight.' Camões has been honoured by titles such as the 'Portuguese Virgil' or the 'Portuguese Plutarch.' Hitherto we shall pursue the evolvement of his epic as it provoked, inspired and engaged writers through the centuries. George Monteiro's meticulous study and assessment in *The Presence of Camões* (UPK, 1996), brings forth Camões's global influence on the writings of eminent literary icons. George writes,

'Introduced to English readers in 1655, Camões's work from the beginning appealed strongly to writers. The young Elizabeth Barrett's Camonean poems, for example, inspired Edgar Allan Poe to appropriate elements from Camões. Herman Melville's reading of Camões bore fruit in his career-long borrowings from the Portuguese poet. Longfellow, T. W. Higginson, and Emily Dickinson read and championed Camões. And Camões as epicist and love poet is an *éminence grise* in several of Elizabeth Bishop's strongest Brazilian poems.

Besides emulating Camões through their varied responses, other scholarships also experimented on an intertextuality of languages by translating *Os Lusíadas*. Its first two English translations by Sir Richard Fanshawe and William Julius Mickle were followed by that of Sir Richard Burton, the adventurer-traveller, writer and translator of *Arabian Nights*. Many more followed through the nineteenth and twentieth century, ending in the latest by Landeg White.

The translation by Landeg White is interesting in the context of Goa, India. By shifting the emphasis from Portuguese adjectives and adverbs to nouns and verbs in the English language, Landeg stripped the epic of its nationalistic fervour, rendering it as the first modern adventure of science and exploration, wrought in Goa. Just as Camões's delineation of the 'Spirit of the Cape of Good Hope' — figured as the mythological Adamastor by him, appears in the writings of Southern African writers Charles Eglington, David Wright and Stephen Gray, so does Landeg White's translation introduce an added context for intercultural studies of *Os Lusíadas* in Goa. In his book *Camões: Made in Goa* (Peepal Tree, 2017), he writes, '*Os Lusíadas* is very much a poem made in Goa, the Goan perspective being fundamental.'

It is indeed fascinating to note that the epic was penned by Camões during his East Indies sojourn. Landeg's argument is that Camões would have just been a mediocre courtly poet had he not been exiled. Struggling to find a novel lyrical idiom when forced to contend with ulterior exotic escapades, as also studying Portugal from an objective lens of exile, Camões arrived at his poetic form for *Os Lusíadas*.

Landeg elaborates, 'Vasco da Gama, doubling for the moment as Camões's narrator, describes to the Sultan of Malindi, the Europe from which he has sailed. It is a passage without precedent in earlier European writing, a vision of Europe as a single historical, geographical, and cultural entity, beginning where Russia borders Asia, and extending across Lapland and Scandinavia, through Poland and Germany, Greece and Italy and France, and finally to Iberia, with Spain the head of Europe and Portugal its crown. This vision has many features, but its key is that this is Europe seen for the first time from outside. More precisely, it is being described from the perspective of India. The whole epic turns on this.'

In his book *Konkani Bhashechem Zoit* (The Triumph of Konkani, 1930), Shennoy Goembab indicates that there is a strong probability that Camões was inspired to write the epic in Goa. The academic Olivinho Gomes is quoted in an interview with Frederick Noronha, 'All these facts go to prove by a preponderance of probability that he wrote the epic or a substantial part of it in Goa, where he wrote most of his poetry.'

There is monumental commemoration of Camões's presence in Goa beginning with a seamount in the Indian Ocean named after Camões. The Archaeological Museum at Old Goa houses a three-meter high bronze statue of Luís de Camões. The statue was originally installed in the garden in 1960 but was moved into the museum due to public protest after Goa's annexation to India. Another Camões monument in Goa, the Jardim de Garcia da Orta Garden, has a 12-meter high pillar in the centre. Additionally, the entrance foyer of Braganza Hall, Panjim, has the grand Azulejos adorning its walls and depicts scenes from *Os Lusíadas*.

Let's now turn the lens to the other end of the spectrum — the children of Goa who grew up reading *Os Lusíadas* in their

school curriculum at the Portuguese Lyceum. They hailed the
epic for its poetic splendour and imagery. It gave them a sense of
identity with the Portuguese. This thought arises from the concept
of 'Lusotropicalism', adopted by the dictator Antonio de Oliviera
Salazar through out the Portugal's overseas colonies. Partially
propagated by the Brazilian sociologist Gilberto Freyre describing
the miscegenation, racial democracy and civilising thrust of the
Portuguese rule, it became a reality in Goa. Simply put, the notion
implied that ethnic tribes were Portuguese — a brotherhood and
respect that sustained a humane coexistence of master-slave unity.

In the postcolonial Lusotropicalist climate in Goa, writers
such as Pandurang Bhangi, Prakash Thali, Ravindra Kelekar,
Manohar Sardessai,[30] Madhavi Sardessai, Olvinho Gomes and Ave
Cleto Afonso have worked assiduously and orchestrated literary
symphonies between European and Indian languages through their
works of scholarship and translation.

In 2003, Goa's man of letters, Olivinho Gomes undertook an
ambitious task of producing a 747-page Konkani translation of
Camões's epic. The highly fulfilling project, mirrored through the
potentiality and opulence of his native tongue, evidences Olvinho's
delight and admiration of the epic. Keeping with his innate wish
to reflect on and render the world's greatest literature in Konkani,
Olivinho weaves parallels between the two tongues, resulting in
strands of *ottava rima* (a form of poetry consisting of stanzas of
eight lines), in Konkani that resonate beautifully with the essence
and beat of the original epic. He further delivered the text in both
the Devanagari and Roman scripts of the language, accomplishing
an indefatigable feat in one literary work.

Inspired by Olivinho's effort, five years down the line Ave Cleto
Afonso undertook a literary project, *O Vaticinio do Swarga* — an

---

30. A collection of original poetry alongside its English translation, and a very useful
introduction by D. A. Smith appeared entitled *Avante, Goeses, Avante: The Portuguese Poetry
of Laxmanrao Sardessai*, Goa, 1556, 2017.

epic in Konkani and Portuguese. The adulation for Camões's epic is very much in place but the Goan ideology has moved from just adulation. Ave Cleto's work is a reparation of psychological scars of cosmetic Lusotropicalism, undergirding colonial domination and repression in Goa. Resting strong on the agency that the pen is mightier than the sword, Ave Cleto generates a dialogue between literatures and languages (Portuguese and Konkani) of ruler and the ruled in order to transform the common friendships between people and civilisation. Drawing on his own Portuguese/Indian duality, the extended title of the book being *'O que Os Lusíadas Nao Canta'* or What Os Lusíadas Does Not Tell You,' Ave Cleto goes on to elucidate the ground reality behind the chimerical master-slave relationship. Landeg hails Ave Cleto's writing as, 'A work in six cantos of *ottava rima,* mixing Portuguese and Konkani, part commentary, part scholarly, it is a labour of love and a resolute rebuttal of Lusophone interpretations of the Indo-Portuguese encounter.' It also features as a prominent text in the extended reading list in Landeg's own book, *Camões: Made in Goa.*

Ave Cleto's esoteric writing scales a landmark with *O Vaticinio Do Swarga* taking Goan literature to a new level. An act of subversive writing undertaken with keen sensitivity and empathy, it disrupts many myths perpetuated by the powerful West. At the end of this journey the subaltern comes into his own and stands tall, naked and proud, resplendent in his history, heritage, language and culture. Appreciating Camões's epicist craftsmanship, Ave Cleto frames his repartee in the same mould, beginning his work with an invocation of Gods of the Hindu mythology. Throwing away phantoms of the past, he etches paths of glory by honouring Indian history and its people. Delineating legends and myths a parallelism emerges between Hindu and Olympian Gods and their meddling in the affairs of man. A river of Konkani and Portuguese streams through civilisational upheavals, according tribute to Indo-Aryan culture but through a Latinate idiom. A lyrical exaltation of the

Indian freedom movement roots its refrain in a freedom song, more precious than any golden cage such as that of Lusotropicalism.

Here a mention of the essay *Milton and Camões: Reinventing the Old Man* by Balachandran Rajan is also befitting. Balachandra, the Miltonic expert, returns to the theme of imperialism and postcolonialism. There is sufficient evidence to suggest that Milton read the Portuguese Camões's epic *The Lusiads* (at least in English translation). John Mulryan from St. Bonaventure University writes, Balachandra pins his argument on the fact that *The Lusiads* is a secular epic that clearly equates commercial and imperial interests. 'The Old Man of Belem,' referred to in the title of the essay functions as a countervoice to Camões's poem, 'arguing that the epic should not be written at all' — that is, the imperialist voyage should be stopped before it begins. At this point, Balachandra touches on his identity as a native Indian whose country was colonised and degraded by commercial imperialists from the West. In a sentence that bears repetition, he notes that in our time so-called objectivity must give way to advocacy: 'We can no longer leave our ideologies in the cloakroom as we enter the literary seminar.'

We all know that collective memory is selective and that it is only possible thanks to a process of selective amnesia. We also know that subaltern identities strive to turn amnesia into memory. When the two meet — in the political-economic and cultural processes of the politics of identity — we have a chance to wake up from anaesthesia and to imagine 'otherselves' and thus make amends not only to historical wrongdoings but also to contemporary inequalities, writes Miguel Vale de Almeida in his essay 'Otherselves.'

Recent works along these lines include the play, 'Os Lusíadas Never Heard Them,' based on a book and audiobook of the same title, written by the actor Antonio Fonseca. It is based on *Os Lusíadas* and explores coincidences with the current time. Goa's queen of fado, Sonia Shirsat has also lent her voice to the project. In

2016, a Malayalam translation by Dr Davees CJ, and supported by Instituto Camões Goa, was released.

Taking these writings into account, we can say that Camões's Os Lusíadas has come a long way. In his essay 'Death of the Author,' French critic and theorist Roland Barthes asserted that books are 'eternally written here and now,' with each reading and critical study. Os Lusíadas has been reinterpreted, recreated and as such reborn — the newer versions making an incisive cut into the veneer of supremacy — the so-called 'white man's burden.' The panoramic view of the East from the East introduces the world to the sight, smells and sounds of a different music in the plains and waters of India, and examines the truths of individuals and events in history, rooting them into alternative realities of this land. Thus intercultural studies involving the epic have opened pathways of understanding and dialogue, and renewed ways of seeing, facilitating a new present.

Endnotes

Young Under the Apple Boughs
Excerpted from *Up and About in Nairobi and Bombay* (2018).
The complete memoir can be read online at the *Joao Roque Literary Journal.*

Matters of the Heart
Excerpted from a novel-in-progress, *The Fires of Gangapur.*

Confluence
First appeared in the *FemAsia Journal,* April 2018.